COMMON GLOBE
OR
GLOBAL COMMONS

BUSINESS ECONOMICS AND FINANCE

a series of monographs and textbooks

Executive Editor
Arthur B. Laffer
Department of Economics
University of Chicago
Graduate School of Business
Chicago, Illinois

Co-Editor
Gene C. Uselton
Department of Economics
Texas Tech University
College of Arts and Sciences
Lubbock, Texas

Throughout recorded history, the science of economics has fascinated and affected more people than perhaps any other discipline short of religion. From the simple process of bartering beads for salt to the vastly complex machinery of modern international trade, the principles and currents of economics lend a hand in shaping our daily lives. It is the aim of this series to illuminate the rapidly expanding horizons of this science—to document and explore the world of commerce and human interdependence.

Volume 1
Common Globe or Global Commons: Population Regulation and Income Distribution   *John C. G. Boot*

Other Volumes in Preparation

COMMON GLOBE
OR
GLOBAL COMMONS

population regulation and income distribution

Johannes Cornelius Gerardus

John C. G. Boot

State University of New York at Buffalo
Buffalo, New York

MARCEL DEKKER, INC.   New York

MARCEL DEKKER, INC.
270 Madison Avenue, New York, New York 10016

LIBRARY OF CONGRESS CATALOG CARD NUMBER: 74-79919
ISBN: 0-8247-6231-2

Current printing (last digit):
10 9 8 7 6 5 4 3 2 1

Printed in the United States of America

Froukje Tjitske Tuinman

1948-1970

Contents

v

Preface

Bird's-Eye View of Book

The first dozen chapters of this book present only a new combination—there is nothing new or original in the ingredients, it is their mixture, dosage, and presentation that makes the new dish. The chapters are short and straight-forward, written with a sense of economy, yet without losing sight of significant detail. Inevitably, there will be much that is redundant for many. The clear labeling of the short sections within each chapter will hopefully enable the reader to skip familiar ground.

The last half-dozen chapters are more novel in content, presenting a fairly detailed plan of population growth regulation on both national and global levels. The proposal's main feature is that it ties the controls to income (re)distribution. At the loss of some flavor, but at little loss of substance, these chapters can be read alone.

Intended Audience

This book is written for everybody. There is virtually nothing that cannot be easily digested by anyone. A large circle of professional colleagues and an even larger circle of friends and interested laymen reviewed various previous versions, and all found it easily understandable, although some found it understandable nonsense.

It is of special interest, however, to economists at the general introductory liberal arts level. One will learn better how to work with economic concepts and what the truly relevant issues are by reading this book than by reading a traditional text devoted to micro-, macro-, or price-theory. This is a useful complement to such texts.

The interests of ecologists and planners might be particularly tickled by this short book, which surveys a number of fashionable topics such as pollution, depletion, population, externalities, and delays, both individually and in interaction. This book has a far more specific population regulation proposal than any other proposal currently available in the market of ideas.

References

A large number of issues are mentioned in passing without full and detailed discussion. Of these, only a very few statements and comments are made that are not elaborated on in some detail in one or more of the following four books, mentioned here in order of importance and relevance to the text:

Ehrlich, Paul R., and Anne H. Ehrlich, *Population, Resources, Environment,* 2nd edition, W. H. Freeman, San Francisco. This book, replete with references, surveys the problems concisely and accurately. It is a rich source of factual data, lucidly presented, happily informative, quietly persuasive.

Boulding, Kenneth E., *The Meaning of the 20th Century*, Harper and Row, New York. This book is more philosophical in nature and wider in scope than the others. Boulding is a philosopher with both feet solidly on the ground, and while his comments soar to great heights of insight, perceptiveness, and originality, his head is not in the clouds. The suggestion of certificates is his brainchild.

Meadows, Donella H., Dennis L. Meadows, Jørgen Randers, and William W. Behrens III, *The Limits To Growth,* A Potomac Associates Book, Universe Books, New York. This book asks the question "Where are we going?" It analyzes that question with potentially extremely useful techniques, and finds that under a vast variety of different assumptions the end is always the same—

a severe contraction of population during the next century, plus assorted other ills and miseries. It should be read with some skepticism, not for what it says but for what it omits to incorporate into its models.

Dales, J. H., *Pollution, Property & Prices*, University of Toronto Press. A very gentle, honest, wise book focusing on pollution and its regulation and written by a professional economist. Chapter 12 is largely derived from this stimulating, thought-provoking book.

All these books are short and eminently readable.

Acknowledgments

I gratefully acknowledge the support of my employer, the State University of New York at Buffalo, and the hospitality of the University of Wyoming in Laramie during the summer months of 1972, and of the University of Massachusetts at Amherst during the autumn of 1972.

Mr. and Mrs. Richard B. Dopkins and Dr. William C. Fischer of Buffalo, N.Y., Dr. George M. Frankfurter of Syracuse, N.Y., and Mr. and Mrs. John Schimmel III of Williamstown, Mass., are among many whose comments on and criticism of earlier versions of this book were much appreciated. A Parisian sister summarily dismissed it all as utterly absurd, an identical twin by contrast thought it all so eminently clear and logical that no comment was needed. There is but one of those.

My wife Hinke and two children Maren and Mark are disappointed because *we* practice what *I* preach, procreation in moderation. I also preach that this is a misguided surrender to moral suasion, a view that becomes more persuasive with the passage of time.

Dedication

Froukje was a sister-in-law, a young lady we loved. She was a victim of someone else's negligence on the road. Our lives are the richer for having shared part of them with her.

John C. G. Boot

COMMON GLOBE
OR
GLOBAL COMMONS

1

The Rule of 70

Doubling Times

The rule of 70 is easy to comprehend, but difficult to fully appreciate. The rule states that if something grows at a rate of x percent per year, it will be twice as much $70/x$ years later. Capital at the savings bank earning 5 percent per year will double in $70/5$ or 14 years. A population growth of 1½ percent per year implies that the population doubles every $70/1½ = 46$ years. If demand for electricity grows at an annual rate of 7 percent, demand will double every decade.

The rule is no quirk—it is a mathematical law which comes about because the natural logarithm of 2 is .6931. More accurate rounding would result in the rule of 69, but this value has been preempted by sexology. Thus it is that we speak of the rule of 70.

This simple rule has staggering consequences. A doubling time of a decade means ten doubling times in a century. *One* original unit doubled ten times gives 2, 4, 8, . . ., 1,024 units, so that *a 7 percent annual increase gives a thousandfold increase over the timespan of a century.* The first decade of that century witnesses an innocuous increase from 1 to 2; the last decade will see an increase from about 500 to about 1,000. This may, or may not, be harmless. If the original unit is your dollar at the savings bank earning 7 percent per year, it is all to the good. If the original unit is household garbage in 1874, and if this garbage increased at 7 percent per year until 1974, the thousand units presently generated could be disturbing.

Compounding

Fortunately, garbage production does not quite grow at the rate of 7 percent per year. A yearly rate of 3 percent is more realistic. Unfortunately, this neither changes the principle nor the long run result; it only changes the length of the long run. A 3 percent annual growth rate implies a doubling time of 23 years, and thus 10 doubling times in 230 years, after which time the original unit has become a thousand units. The rule of 70 makes, *in time,* thousands out of units; and in *twice* as much time millions out of units and in *thrice* as much time billions out of units. This is the terror of compound interest, the danger of exponential growth.

Application of Compounding

In 1624 the Dutch reputedly paid the Indians $24 for Manhattan Island. If this sum had been invested at 7 percent per year, the kitty would have grown to over 800 billion dollars in 1974, that is, 350 years and 35 doubling times later. This amount is rather more than its actual value today. However, a less astute investment earning only 5 percent per year would have resulted in a total of around 800 million dollars in 1974, which would still be 350 years, but now only 25 doubling times, later. This amount is rather less than its actual value today. In the long run a small difference (7 percent versus 5 percent) makes a big difference (billions versus millions).

Discounting

Similarly, $24 in 1974, if invested at 7 percent per year, would be over $800 billion in 2324, which in 1974 is as far in the future as 1624 is in the past. Another way of looking at this is that the promise of receiving $800 billion in 2324 is worth only about $24 today, when discounted at the going rate of 7 percent.

Such discounting of future values has profound implications. It effectively limits the view to a rather close horizon, a timespan of 20 years or so. A potential profit of $10 million 50 years hence is worth but $75,000 today when discounted at the more or less typical rate of 10 percent. Thus it is that profits turn into peanuts. A potential liability of $10 million 50 years hence features on to-day's balance sheet at $75,000, because it is discounted at 10 percent. Thus it is that substantial liabilities turn into comparative trivialities.

Short-Run Vision

Discounting generates a short-run vision. High discounting generates myopic vision: only those investments will be made which are profitable in the short run. The long-run, growth-oriented types of investment (roads, energy supply, education), the fruits of which will be reaped in the far future, will be neglected because high discounting has wiped out their present value.

The true state of affairs is even more ominous, because the concentration on instant profitability will inevitably frustrate future growth—whether by whaling to the hilt, or by building to-day the *slums,* instead of the *houses,* for tomorrow. The right road is found by fixing one's eyes on the far horizon, rather than by focusing on tomorrow's profit.

This far horizon, to be sure, is not infinitely far. It is hard to really care about what will be in the year 2500, let alone the year 9000. A period of 200 years will include the full life of all grand-children. Moreover, all planning becomes pure guesswork after some length of time, after which it should be heavily discounted. A discount rate of 1 or 2 percent effectively limits the horizon to a span of one or two centuries. At 1½ percent, what will be 200 years hence is considered only about one-tenth as important as what will happen next year. That seems eminently reasonable.

2

Population

Current Population Growth Rate

Population is governed by the rule of 70. Currently it grows, on a global basis, at a rate of about 2 percent per year, which amounts to nearly 200,000 a day. This implies a doubling time of $70/2 = 35$ years. Someone in the late thirties today lives on a globe twice as densely populated as the day (s)he was born. A doubling time of 35 years results in an eightfold increase in a century, plus some odd years. Imagine the year 2080 with eight bodies for every one today, two or three houses for every one today, and so on.

A Nonsense Fantasy

At such a rate of progression Adam and Eve all by themselves would, beginning at the year zero, have generated the world's present population of 4 billion around the year 1100. This was the year when the Christians, just returning from their first crusade, were unlocking the chastity belts of their chatelaines, lest the reproductive process pause too long.

Adam's and Eve's offspring today would be 50 million times our current population, or more than 3 million per square mile of land—strictly standing room only. About 70 years later the oceans would be just as crowded as the land, and the next generation would see us packed like Portuguese sardines, or jammed like Japanese train commuters. In a matter of a few thousand years the expanse of the galaxy would be vacuum-sealed with an amorphous mass of mankind.

Checks on Growth

But all this is just nonsense. Utter, unadulterated nonsense. If every codfish egg became cod, we would have Atlantic Cod instead of Atlantic Ocean within a decade. In fact, the number of cod is controlled by checks such as a limited amount of space, food, and cannibalistic appetites, so there is no danger whatever in their overtaking the oceans.

Human population growth is subjected to similar checks, although some of these, disease and infant mortality, have become vastly less effective with simple measures of hygiene and the progress of medicine. This, in fact, largely explains the very high current growth rate of 2 percent—we have a form of death control without an equally efficient form of birth control.

Other checks, space and food, will become and to some extent already are operative to limit growth as growth proceeds. Less obvious but equally important may be psychological checks, such as stress and neuroses. Belligerent checks of war and wanton slaughter are not beyond the realm of imagination, or the realm of reality, for that matter. But it is useful to devise ways to somehow limit growth by more sensible techniques than crowding and starving, psychoses and warring.

Finite Growth

Historically, the growth rate has been much lower than 2 percent: the extrapolation of that figure into the indefinite future, therefore, is wholly unwarranted. However, this is relatively small solace, since any positive population growth rate will, in time, double and redouble and re-redouble the population. If the globe can support but a finite number, growth will have to stop at some stage. One can debate forever what this finite number is, even as one can debate forever whether there is more nourishment in the hole of a doughnut or the fragrance of Camembert cheese. Such debate is vacuous. What counts is the principle that, since the universe cannot provide for an infinite number, the number by necessity is finite. Since it is finite, it cannot forever grow— asymptotic limits aside. Since it cannot forever grow, growth must at some point stop.

Zero Growth Rate and Average Lifetime

When the growth rate is zero, the population is level. This implies that there will be an equal number of births and deaths each year. It could be equal, however, at various levels. One could have 10 deaths and births per thousand per year, or 20, or 25, or x. For those who enjoy life it is quite important where the value is, because the average life span is equal to $1{,}000/x$ years.

Thus, if there are 20 births and deaths per thousand per year, the average lifetime is inevitably and unavoidably $1{,}000/20 = 50$ years. For a value of 14 births and deaths per thousand per year the average lifetime would be $1{,}000/14 = 71$ years, less than the present life expectancy in Holland or Hungary.

The actual number of births per thousand per year varies widely from country to country, and from time to time in the same country. At present no country has as few as 14 births per thousand per year, although some European countries very closely approach that level. In North America and Russia the value is presently below 16. In South America it is around 40, in some African countries it exceeds 50. *If* the populations in those countries were stable, the average lifetime would be less than 20 years. It would be little consolation for the loved ones left behind that everybody everywhere always dies too early, in the sense that the actuarially expected age at which one dies is always positive.

3

Pollution

Omnipresent Pollution

Pollution is the inevitable by-product of both production and consumption. An economy which, using the same technology, produces twice as many shoes and twice as many tomatoes will produce twice as much pollution. The consumption of this production will in turn generate its own pollution. Consumed tomatoes will end up as sewage, consumed shoes as household garbage or, worse yet, litter. We do not need any Midas touch to guarantee that all we touch will, eventually, turn into garbage.

Cyclical Transformation of Products

In the vast majority of cases producers and consumers are but *transformers*. Production does not create anything out of a vacuum, nor does anything vanish into nothingness after consumption. Producer-transformers take from the earth a large menu of matter, such as trees, whales, and water. To these matters they add energy, which is also largely taken from the earth in the form of coal, oil, or gas. With the help of a third ingredient, know-ledge or know-how, they transform these materials into an astonish-ingly rich variety of *goods* (lampshades and lifevests, crosses and coffins) and an often overlooked but very real component of *bads*, such as slag piles, noise, and heat.

Consumer-transformers change the goods into garbage and sewage, flyash and nitrogen oxides, and proceed to discard these back into the environment. It is a never ending cycle of trans-formations creating a perpetuum mobile of polluting matter.

Surplus Industry

The most important exception to this cyclical view is pro-vided by the knowledge, or educational, industries. In these industries, something is created more or less out of nothing into what is more or less a vacuum. A previously empty information storage center in the brain is filled with some information, which, when it later disappears with passage of time or in death, does so without polluting. At the end of a class, some know more without anyone knowing less. In this sense education is a surplus industry, even though some information may never be productive or may in point of fact be wrong.

By contrast, most other industries are deficit industries. To see this, consider what the production of a 1940 automobile does to the present system. Nothing good and some bad. The car is long evaporated, rusted, and jettisoned. The steel and other materials that went into making it is no longer even potentially useful. The gas that car once used is irretrievably lost. So the globe is the worse for the car having been produced. A similar story can be told for virtually all industries other than those designed to teach, whether they teach algebra, the gospel, swimming, or pickpocketing.

Recycling

The cyclical view of pollution illustrates forcefully that any element, in one shape and place and time a resource, is a pollutant later in the cycle when it has a different shape or place. The most spectacular example of such a place is outer space. Less than two decades post-Sputnik, space is filled with human artifacts and dead mice, referred to as space-junk. This junk cycles forever and ever in a very literal sense, but is not being recycled. The deep ocean bottom now stores dangerous gases next to sunken ships. The wide ocean surface is now covered in sticky slicks of oil, more likely to be struck by red snappers than oil prospectors. The highest mountain in Houston is composed of garbage—most of which might have been recycled to make compost.

Today's pollutants are yesterday's resources out of shape and place. By recycling we try to make today's pollutants into tomorrow's resources. We do not need to return to the honeybucket way of recycling human waste to the pastures, but we could return to the disposal of sewage on land, where it fertilizes, rather than in streams and lakes, where it pollutes.

The cyclical and interacting view of pollution also brings home the point that it is fatuous to divide mankind into two groups: mean polluters and noble pollutees. We are all guilty, and we are all victims. We are *also* all profiteers when we eat wormless, because pesticide-sprayed, fruits, and when we pay less for electricity because the generator does not clean up its foul smoke.

Growth of Pollution

Over the long haul industrialized countries increase output at a rate of 3 percent per year. Hence the doubling time is roughly $70/3 = 23$ years, implying a twentyfold increase in production over the span of a century. Pollution in fact increased at a faster rate, because advancing technology replaced relatively clean labor with relatively dirty machines. All told, a thirtyfold increase in pollution over the last century is a good ballpark figure for the United States.

Multiplicative Interaction

Another way of deriving this value of 30 is instructive. First, during the last century the population grew threefold. Second, the per capita production grew roughly six- or sevenfold, so that the total production grew twentyfold—three times as many people producing nearly seven times as much per person. Third, the pollution per unit of production grew by a factor of around 1½. Total pollution, therefore, grew about thirtyfold—twenty times as much production and 1½ times as much pollution per unit of production. The point to note is that while the values 3, 6 or 7, and 1½ are all rather moderate, their multiplicative interaction $3 \times$ (6 or 7) $\times$ (1½) = 30 gets us to an awesome total.

Though none of these multiples can be very precisely determined, the value 1½ must be viewed with particular skepticism.

Whatever its value now, this figure may decline in the future, both because of public and political concern about pollution, and because of a slow but steady shift away from pollution-intensive industrial and agricultural commodities to pollution-extensive service commodities: health services, educational services, recreational services. Such a decline would be very useful. The value 30 would become 20 if 1½ were to become 1.

4

Natural Resources

Minerals

There is no cause for complacency where natural resources are concerned. Although estimates vary wildly and are frequently revised, it is conceded that the amount of *known and economically harvestable* reserves of many minerals is quite small. In one set of estimates the known aluminum supply at the current rate of usage will last us for another 160 years, the copper supply for 40, the lead for 20 years. If the rate of usage of these minerals were to increase by 2½ percent per year, these values would be deflated to 65, 28, and 17 years, respectively.

To be sure, for the right price nearly everything can be had in quantities far exceeding foreseeable future needs. Rocks, oceans, and the earth's core are veritable treasure chests of minerals. The limits are therefore primarily economic (rather than physical) in nature, and the words "economically harvestable" are the operative ones. What is not economical now may well become economical

14

as prices rise or new harvesting techniques and energy sources are developed.

Fuels

The present supply of fuels such as crude oil, natural gas, and uranium is already tight, making for a tense situation. The currently known deposits of each of these fuels will be exhausted in 20 to 30 years. In the developed Western and Japanese economies the imbalance between the local supply—which could perhaps be stretched to last until 1980—and local demand is particularly acute. The specter of regular brownouts interspersed with occasional blackouts is no longer confined to nightmares. Flights are occasionally cancelled for lack of fuel—although suspicion still lingers that lack of passengers may be a factor contributing to the cancellation. Gas stations are occasionally out of gas, although some deliberate effort of the big companies to drive the independents out of business may be no total stranger to the cause. Houses are occasionally cold, although this may be due in some degree to distribution problems.*

Of all current sources of energy—and these current sources are nothing else than stored up solar energy of days gone by—only coal is more amply available. Unfortunately, coal tends to pollute more than oil or gas.

---

*These last few lines, written in January 1973, need no further emphasis today. The word "occasionally" should be replaced by "regularly" throughout. If it was ever true that the airline industry could discern a silver lining in the cloud of scarcity, that no longer appears true. The time to believe that the big oil companies are playing games has also passed, although the ethics and perspicacity of their managements remains a matter of debate.

Predatory Economies

The developed nations in general require so much importing of fuels and ores from the less developed nations, that they can justly be characterized as predatory. In using up these stored resources, which were hundreds of millions of years in the making, in just a few decades, the present generation acts as if the world belongs to them. We might not be so sanguine if we were to ponder that it might be more nearly correct to say that we belong to the world.

Until as recently as a century ago this world was essentially as we found it when we arrived. Our impact on resources and ecological systems was not much greater than that of ants or elephants, much less than that of earthquakes or volcanic eruptions, and trivial compared with the impact of ice-ages. Metaphorically speaking, the earth was virginal.

In this last century we are raping the virgin, fast and furious. She is very seductive. Scratching, pounding, tapping, and molesting her gives us all sorts of goodies, from water and wood to gold and diamonds. "They will strip her naked and leave her desolate; they will batten on her flesh and burn her to ashes . . . All nations have drunk deep of the fierce wine of her fornication, the kings of the earth have committed fornication with her and merchants the world over have grown rich on her bloated wealth." The Bible, especially out of context, is always a good provider of quotes.

Air

Man does not live by minerals and fuels alone. Until recently man hardly lived by minerals and fuels at all. Man lives by air, water, and bread.

Air is plentiful, although it can locally be extremely polluted to the point of being at *some* times an immediate and definite health hazard for all, and at *all* times a slow and surreptitious messenger of death in the form of lung diseases for some. The wide and constant circulation of the air dissipates local pollutants in most cases so widely that only regional problems persist. This is, of course, bad enough if you happen to be in the polluted region, since there is no really practical alternative to breathing the air around you. Polluted air also has a hearty appetite for cathedrals, which visibly deteriorate in a matter of years after centuries of durable stability. Unlike lungs, cathedrals cannot pick up and run.

A somewhat exceptional case is that of airborne radiation pollution, where warning bells ring far from the generating source in both distance and time. There is a direct relationship between the amount of radiation (roentgen) and the frequency of "spontaneous" mutations produced in the genes. This is a fancy way of saying that the probability of birth defects increases with increasing radiation.

Climate

The real problems with air are the long-run effects of the slow and gradual pollution of the globe's atmosphere. These effects, in isolation and combination, are largely unknown. They all have in common that they influence the earth's ability to absorb or reflect sunlight, and, therefore, the earth's climate. The gradual increase of finely divided particulate matter can have severe repercussions for the global climates, as Krakatoa and other vomiting volcanoes of the past have shown.

In the last decade a 30 percent increase in atmospheric dust particles has been recorded at remote poles and high mountain posts. Much of this is due to industry and transportation, and even more is due to agricultural pesticides. Whatever the source or composition, the gradual increase of dustiness may well create climatic disturbances by slowly transforming the earth into one giant greenhouse, unable to radiate heat back into space. King penguins will be sweating it out as the South Pole becomes a Finnish sauna. The injection of water vapor in the stratosphere by jets also has consequences for the planet's radiative potential. How these effects will combine and what the overall effect will be is unknown.

Nor is air pollution the only potential source to play havoc with climate and climate patterns. Much of the energy we use is eventually dissipated in heat and radiated into space. At present the sun is more than 10,000 times as great a heat producer as human activities, but in 10 doubling times—that is a thousandfold increase—the sun is more powerful by a factor of 10 only. That would certainly dramatically heat the climate and melt the ice-caps. Ten doubling times will require less than two centuries at the present yearly growth rate of 4 percent in energy use. Already the cities are heat islands. If we succeed in opening the earth's core to tap the heat we may well be opening Pandora's box. As so often is the case, solution of one problem—energy scarcity—creates other problems—heat dissipation. The solution becomes the problem. The solution to the problem of codling moths turned into the problem of red mites whose numbers used to be controlled by preying codling moths.

On top of all this there is some deliberate effort on the part of man to influence the weather, mainly by the device of cloud seeding. Rather unsuccessful so far, it is not without interesting potential. It is also not without potential conflicts of interest. The rain seeded in Colorado will not fall in Iowa, even as the

Colorado river tapped to irrigate Colorado will not irrigate California. The wanton arbitrariness of the vagaries of weather may be preferable, on this count alone, to deliberate human intervention helping some but hurting others.

Water

Water, though continuously recycled by evaporation (one of the important contributions of solar energy to the global system), condensation, and precipitation is already a bottleneck in many areas, and getting scarcer by the day. Direct human consumption for drinking, washing, and cleaning may, in the United States, average out to no more than a few hundred or so gallons per person per day. Direct use for lawns and pools increases this value substantially, perhaps to five hundred gallons a day.

The real villain, however, is the *indirect* use of water, which is nearly wholly unperceived although it is so large that the average use of water per person per day is well above 1,500 gallons. It takes about 100 gallons of water to produce a pound of wheat, 5,000 gallons of water to produce a pound of beef, 100,000 gallons of water to produce a car, 500,000 gallons of water to produce a ton of synthetic rubber, and 1,600,000 gallons of water to irrigate one acre of farmland for one season. In consuming a two-pound steak the family unwittingly consumes 10,000 gallons of water, give or take a few thousand gallons.

Unlike air, water is unevenly distributed over the globe, as a consequence of uneven distribution of rainfall and the very pronounced tendency of water to flow downhill. This uneven distribution makes desert wastelands of wide areas of real estate, and mosquito-breeding marshlands elsewhere.

Problem of the Commons

Air and water belong to the class of resources which every one is permitted to use, but for which no one takes particular responsibility. Whales belong to the same class of commodities, as do national parks. Such commodities tend to be overused and undernourished. If whales could speak, they could tell quite a story about that.

This phenomenon of overuse and undernourishment is known as the problem of the commons. The English village in the olden days used to have a communal pasture ground, the commons, for the cattle of the villagers. Not only was every villager *allowed* to freely use this resource, every villager *did* use it. Bringing your cow to the commons had a clear advantage to you (your cow was fed) and a very small disadvantage to you (all your other cows on the commons faced a little stiffer competition). Of course, other people's cows also faced a little stiffer competition. The *overall* effect of your extra cow might thus very well be detrimental, but the effect on *you* was beneficial, and that is what counts in *your* decisions.

Of late, authorities and governments are formulating rules and regulations limiting some uses of such commons, and thus preventing some of the worst excesses and most serious damage. Pollution, whaling, and national park use are in the process of being regulated.

Food

Food, yearly harvested though it may be—again courtesy of solar energy which transforms carbon dioxide by photosynthesis

into organic molecules which are the beginning of *all* food chains—
is also a scarce resource. Part of the problem is related to a taste or
culture preference for animal protein. Animal protein is one step
further down along the food chain than plant protein, and therefore very inefficient. The animal itself needs around 75 percent of
its consumption of plant protein to stay alive and produce whatever produce it is meant to produce, whether eggs, milk, wool, or
meat. (The largest animals, whales and elephants, consume exclusively plankton and grasses, both first in the food chain.) Part
of the problem is related to the difficulty of storing, transporting,
and distributing food efficiently.

A major problem is the absence of economic demand, a
euphemistic way of saying that the poor and hungry have no cold
cash to pay the price, and a very poor credit rating to boot. We are
approaching the point, however, where even a utopian global
society would be faced with an absolute scarcity of food. Every
additional person bites from two sides: he eats food and infringes
upon the areas for food production, inasmuch as he also needs
Lebensraum. With 200,000 new mouths to feed every day, the
crunch is on.

Comforting Thoughts?

Minerals, fuels, air, water, and food all pose serious problems.
It may be thought comforting that new supplies will be found, or
that substitutes may be developed such as fission and fusion for energy supply, and plankton-pies and algae-cookies for food supply,
much as artificial fertilizers were developed just as Chile's supply of
fossiled bird-droppings and saltpeter was about to be exhausted
and dire predictions of impending famine were a dime a dozen.

It may be thought comforting that resources will be recycled and reused more aggressively as they become scarcer and more expensive, such as recycling aluminum cans or using the same water over and over again, much as the water of the Rhine is tapped, used, and returned an average of five times before it finally flows into the North Sea.

It may be thought comforting that new economical extraction processes might be developed which will vastly increase our supply. After all, optimists may argue, each cubic mile of ocean contains 19 tons of lead, and there are 300 million such cubic miles. And the earth's core contains rich minerals as well as geothermal energy, currently tapped in Klamath Falls, Oregon, and a few but fast-growing number of widely scattered places around the globe.

It may be thought comforting that new inventions can easily make mockeries out of the most scientific crystal-ball-gazing. A technological breakthrough such as the transistor not only miniaturizes, it also saves incredible amounts of energy. Computers, transistors, lasers, surely we have not seen the end of a remarkable series of inventions.

When all is said and done, however, even a hundredfold increase in all of these resources leaves the total amount available strictly finite. Furthermore, at current usage and technology the economically harvestable resources of oil, gas, uranium, tin, silver, zinc, gold, platinum, lead, and mercury will all be exhausted within a quarter of a century, well before the year 2000. The timely development of substitutes and alternatives is not helped by the short-run vision generated by high discount rates.

Limits of Growth

In view of the strictly finite amounts available, it is tempting, but somewhat deceptive, to conclude in more or less absolute terms that there exists such a thing as a limit of growth. This is a deceptive statement when we do not simultaneously emphasize its inverse: the growth of limits. The history of mankind is essentially nothing but a story of the growth of limits. Yet, the lessons of history are extrapolated only at one's peril, and in an absolute, mathematical, logical sense growth cannot forever proceed. The globe has but a finite mass.

At the present juncture it would perhaps be more accurate to speak of limiting growth, in that it is easy to view current growth as limiting not so much the potential for further growth in numbers and quantity, but the potential for further growth in depth and development.

5

Mankind

Better Collective Quality

A special resource worth mentioning separately is mankind itself. This resource is recycled every 50 years or so, with virtually completely nonoverlapping sets every 100 years. This turnover of human capital is expensive, the more so the faster the turnover.

Over the last few centuries improved sanitation, nutrition, and medication have greatly increased the expected lifetime and improved the health of man. We stand a little taller. Menstruation begins a little earlier and ends somewhat later. The fastest skaters skate a little faster. The highest jumpers jump a little higher. All this may or may not be advantageous, but as indicators of better health they tell a tale.

Better health and longer life are a clear blessing from virtually all points of view, in particular from the crass, commercial point of view that it is cheaper to train 2 people for 50 years of productive life than 5 for 20 years of productive service. The quantity and quality of knowledge embodied in the brains of the living is larger than ever. As a collective, mankind has improved in quality.

Apart from medical services, many other services appear to have improved in quality. It appears that laws are juster and judges better. It appears that education is more widespread and that schools are better equipped. It appears that religions are less eager to crusade with swords, more eager to crusade with words. All that is to the good, although there is ample room for further improvement. Selective enforcement is a grave weakness of judicial systems, unequal opportunity is a grave weakness of educational systems, and dogmatic reasoning is a grave weakness of religious systems.

No Better Individual Quality

It cannot be said, however, that man as an individual has improved over time. The qualities of mind—imagination, thought, memory—do not appear to have grown. The defects of mind—cruelty, delusion, greed—are with us as much as ever. Compassion and tolerance remain in short supply. Rulers are not more humane, people not happier, homes not more peaceful, neighbors not more forgiving, clowns not more humorous. Boredom as evidenced by the boob-tube syndrome, restlessness as evidenced by aimless driving from no place in particular to no place in particular and back, lack of purpose as evidenced by an escapist drug culture, and lack of self-discipline as evidenced by swinging sex habits are no improvements over Roman bread and circuses. The problem of enjoying leisure time by being productively idle is not solved, the problem of how to pursue happiness is as elusive as ever. Those who cope well in the art of making a living are often bad in the art of living itself. All in all, the human value system has not improved.

The human body has not further evolved. With medical knowledge no longer allowing for the automatic application of the survival of the fittest, or rather the demise of the weakest, the gene-pool deteriorates as time proceeds, even apart from radiation effects. Natural selection has become rather artificial and somewhat arbitrary.

On the plus side, medical science or serendipity may be inventive or lucky enough to create even more inventive progenitors by prenatal hormonal injections or some such technique. As long as such medical procedures work across the board and are in nature no different from providing pregnant women with extra vitamins and iron, it would be very helpful and would create few moral problems.

Eugenics

An across-the-board improvement of the human race by better and smarter prenatal and postnatal care should not be confused with *eugenics*. In the gentle meaning of that emotionally loaded word, eugenics is directed towards the repair of, or non-reproduction of, genetically determined defects. In practice, this is by no means easy, because usually hereditary diseases and defects are carried by recessive genes. This implies that the carriers of these genes are not identifiable on sight, and are often themselves blissfully unaware of these defects. One would need to trace the family tree and know the medical histories of the forbears to be able to identify the carriers of diseased genes.

Even when used in this sense, eugenics poses legitimate and significant philosophical and ethical issues for society at large, and acutely painful and practical problems for those who know that their genes harbor a high probability of handicapped offspring.

Euthenics

Eugenics has a second and more ominous meaning when used as synonym for *euthenics*: the improvement of the human race, that is, the creation of more intelligent, creative, talented people by selective breeding techniques and genetic tinkering. Such methods work very well for cattle and corn, racehorses and roses, turkeys and tulips. They do not work so well for people.

One obvious obstacle is that, while it may make sense to encourage mating of the better and discourage mating of the poorer of both sexes, it is by no means clear who is better and who is poorer. Who is to judge what the desirable characteristics are, who is to judge which persons possess these characteristics? What is the standard of human excellence, the genetic blueprint of perfection?

Artificial insemination via sperm banks, on a voluntary basis, is a useful option for some couples, but as a systematic way to create a human super race it must be rejected. Indeed, the very notion of a human super race is as deplorable as the fiction that we are all equal. We are all different, but we cannot be measured or appraised along a one-dimensional axis scaled from bad via average and good to super.

This is the difference with racehorses, tulips, or cows, where attention is essentially focused upon one characteristic: fast running, purity of color, or lean steaks. Even when one is interested in more than one characteristic, such as milk *and* meat, one can measure along *one* common axis, money. But how can one compare compassion with intelligence, humor with industriousness, or athletic with artistic ability?

Increasing Numbers

As mankind increases in numbers, our common globe is becoming a global commons. Just as an English farmer saw nothing wrong with adding an extra cow to the commons, so an Earthly family sees nothing wrong with adding an extra person to the globe. At the outset, or in sparsely settled regions, a new person may be to the solid advantage of the existing society as a whole. More people will permit a better division of labor and greater productivity. However, the population nearly always continues to increase until long after it has ceased to bestow a net advantage upon society as a whole. The model of the commons is at work.

Decentralized Decision-Making

One can also recognize in this somewhat weird result one instance, out of many, where decentralized decisions don't lead to an overall optimum. Any top manager who delegates and thereby decentralizes decisions has as a major problem how to guarantee that the decisions made at lower levels serve the objectives of the whole system. This problem is by no means solved, but managers ranging from foremen to Presidents struggle with it continuously and wittingly, if not always successfully. They design and construct all kinds of rules and regulations in their effort to have the interests of the parts keep in step with the interest of the whole.

Where population is concerned, there is no authority and there are no sets of rules to have the interests of the nation, or indeed of the globe, served by what is in the best interest of the individual decision-makers, that is, the individual families. This is no inadvertent oversight, for it is explicitly recognized that in this case optimality should suffer to preserve freedom of decision for the individual families. A point may come where some individual freedom must be sacrificed in the interest of not straying too far from what is best for all.

6

Externalities

Laissez Faire

While the *growth rate* of pollution is largely determined by the growth rate in population and standard of living, the *level* of pollution is inflated due to the pervasive, pernicious influence of externalities. There is an old, stubborn theorem in economics that, if in an economy of pure and perfect competition everyone is allowed to fend for himself, that is, to make those decisions and take those actions which most enhance his own welfare without control or interference, then the system as a whole produces the "maximum" "welfare"—"maximum" in the Pareto sense that nobody can get better off without making someone else worse off, and "welfare" in the material, or even materialistic, sense. This may be referred to as the *laissez faire* rule. As an example of this rule in operation: everyone is free to choose his own way to reach downtown in the morning rush hour.

Under a number of heroic assumptions, most of which are patently unrealistic and invariably violated in practice, this is true. One of these assumptions is the liberal fiction that everybody knows his own best interest. Another assumption abstracts from indivisibilities (try flying half a plane) and increasing returns to scale (try producing cars at a rate of 10 a year). Violation of these assumptions frustrates the proper functioning of competition and marginality conditions. Yet another assumption prescribes perfect transparency of all markets to all (try to find out the price of prescription medicine at two neighboring drugstores if you have any illusions on this score). This last assumption is even more stringent than at first sight it appears, for it implies that the future is also transparent, or at least that whatever uncertainty there is is marketable as an insurance contract, in a futures market, or transferable to others (the Government, in practice).

This lack of perfect information makes the *laissez faire* rule, by which all motorists may freely choose their own way down-town, not optimal. This is the reason why helicopters give traffic reports during rush hours: with perfect information the hope is that the system will tangle itself out as efficiently as possible.

Examples of Externalities

In the present context the most important assumption is that your actions and decisions do not have *externalities*, that is, spillover effects or repercussions for outsiders. In our society, this is hardly ever true. Whether you smoke a cigarette, drive a car, let your weeds grow, turn on the radio, or brush your teeth electrically—all seemingly innocuous and wholly legal behavior—externalities abound. Your smoking fouls up the air for others; your driving does the same and interferes, often lethally, with others; your weeds will find fertile soil next door and even miles away; your radio will be heard by others, and your use of electricity for the laudable purpose of cleaning your teeth dirties the laundry of others living near the electric generator plant. For none of these effects do you pay anything whatever to anyone. The social costs are completely disregarded in the private computations.

By contrast, you receive nothing from neighbors for maintaining an immaculately cultivated garden with blooming flowers and sweet smells for all nearby to enjoy, or for wearing a pretty necktie or a daring Dior creation. The social benefits are also disregarded in private computations. In the presence of externalities, striving for private gain without minding social welfare does not automatically lead to maximum welfare. We conclude that, despite the helicopters, the traffic need not be Pareto optimal, for traffic has many externalities. (In particular, private automobile traffic has many other undesirable externalities: it is a voracious consumer of mineral resources and fuels, it is extraordinarily demanding of space, it is a heavy contributor to pollution, and it is so persistent and effective a killer and maimer that the ravages of war fade by comparison.)

Two Psychological Observations

A more subtle externality of the striving for private gain by individual competitiveness as prescribed by *laissez faire* is not without dangers. Competition, whether for grades or money or women or whatever, makes every man the potential enemy of his neighbor. A winner implies a loser. Thus, while in theory it "maximizes" "welfare," it should not be even jocularly suggested that *laissez faire* is also the design to create maximum happiness. Such happiness, however elusive a concept that may be, is more a function of the division or distribution of the production than of the total amount of production itself.

Psychological spillovers are by no means few. They are the driving force behind many human actions and interactions. The new car Mr. Jones bought has noticeable repercussions for all the neighbors, and Mr. Jones, with whom neighbors have proverbial trouble keeping up, may well have bought that car for his surreptitious pleasure in seeing others go through the quixotic quivers so characteristic of suppressed jealousy.

Individual Externalities Combined

In particularly ironic but by no means infrequent instances, individual externalities may come back with a vengeance. One man brushing his teeth electrically is not going to make much difference, but thousands electrically caring for clean teeth may overload the system and trigger a power failure painful much beyond the inconvenience of brushing one's teeth manually. It is in this sense that infinitely small things may become infinitely important.

Similarly, individually speaking, one whale in the ship's belly is better than 10 in the ocean. Collectively speaking, everybody's one whale may spell the end of a species, as well as the inglorious death of an industry.

(The mildly paradoxical feature of these problems is illustrated by the prisoners' dilemma game. This game is a simple but powerful device to show that in some situations two persons acting in their collective best interest can get to a much better position than the one they could reach by each individually pursuing their own best interest. What is true for two persons holds, in the situations sketched here, also for many.)

For such infinitesimally small, individual externalities which can combine to produce terrifyingly large, total effects unwanted even by the individuals themselves, an enforceable system of regulations is needed. Thus, the whalers should and do limit the size of their catch. That these limits are too high and not easy to police does not negate the principle. In times of water scarcity some uses (sprinkling lawns, filling pools, washing cars) are forbidden. In such instances most people are willing to cooperate and obey, provided all others do.

Premium on Noncompliance

There is a catch here. In many cases those people who do not obey the regulation reap extra benefits. You can safely catch whales to your heart's content if nobody else does, you can happily water the lawn with sufficient pressure provided nobody else does. This premium on noncompliance if everybody else does comply makes it imperative that the regulation be enforceable and be in fact enforced—by law, by agreement, by peer pressure, or by whatever means—but anyway enforced with but minimum slippage. This is the principle underlying forced unionization, because freeloading would give everybody the benefit of the union if everybody *else* joined. This is also the proposition underlying the idea that individually wise actions, brushing teeth electrically or watering lawns, can be collectively stupid. Individual rationality can be collectively irrational.

Let Us Have a Baby

There is one individual decision which has extraordinarily large externalities. The repercussions for outsiders of your having a child are very large indeed, because there are so very many outsiders with whom the child will interact during his lifetime. For the poor in poor countries every baby is one more mouth to feed, and thus a little less food for the others. For the rich in rich countries every child needs a place in school, and later a place to park his car, and yet later his own little plot or piece of property. All across the board, a newborn baby is destined to interact with so many others in so many ways that the externalities generated are vastly more important than the internal effects on the parents who made (or stumbled into) the decision in the first place.

Having children can be a happy and wholesome experience for all in the family, and yet be collectively deplorable. There is stark irony in this tragedy—that good forces and decent people with honorable intentions might produce a world crisis. We no longer need the evil powers of viruses, or the mean men of war, or the brute force of an earthquake, to create a crisis.

Externalities Received

The pervasiveness of small-scale, individually generated externalities will become even more evident when looked at not from the point of view of what externalities we create by smoking a cigarette or wearing a red tie, but which externalities we receive;

that is, to what extent are we influenced by and subjected to, one way or the other, the actions and decisions of others totally removed from us? The truth is that all day long we are the victims, or profiteers, of decisions made wholly by others. One can think of the TV-programming schedule, but the effects can also be very indirect and hidden. The effects can be of the for-want-of-a-nail type. Unexpected guests make a housewife hurry out for coffee. She bumps into you. You drop a soapbottle. A child slips over the slippery soap and breaks a leg. All this, because some people decided to pay an unexpected visit. That was not the decision of the boy with the broken leg.

As society becomes more complicated and interdependent, one man or a small group of men can create havoc for thousands, as happens when someone calls in a bomb-threat, or the wrong lever is pulled at the generator. In an organized society, millions are at the mercy of one. "Never did so few do such harm to so many" may be the watchword of the next generation. Conversely, one is at the mercy of millions, as can be verified in trying to cross a busy main street.

Industrial Externalities

The small-scale externalities generated by each of us individually have their large-scale counterpart in industry, where many social costs do not enter the private computations and where maximum profit is the *Leitmotiv* of managerial decisions. A paper factory discharges its filthy water into a river, a steel plant emits a colorful smokescreen, a bottling plant gladly uses disposable bottles, a mining company is lackadaisical about the health of its miners, a generating plant generates soot as well as electricity. This is all quite legal, but collectively these social costs of private enterprise are substantial.

In some specific cases, where the cause-and-effect relation is quite clear and the damage monetary—supersonic booms splintering windows—the law recognizes that the damage must be paid for by its perpetrator. But in most cases this is not feasible, because the damage is too widely and obscurely spread, and often is not monetary in nature but takes the form of unpleasant smells, irritating noises, unsightly litter, unswimmable water, or strontium-'enriched' milk.

In other cases the spillover is not so much an unhappy though largely unavoidable by-product of a profitable and useful economic activity, but rather is quite deliberately perpetrated in the pursuit of profit. One can think of cyclamate-sweetened coke or stilbestrol-fattened steers—both possibly carcinogenic substances, and certainly no health foods. In such cases the law can simply forbid the spillover.

Coping with Industrial Externalities

For large-scale industrial or agricultural externalities, a change from private to social accounting to internalize many of these external costs would substantially reduce the pollution level. However, the practical difficulties of such an approach are such that in fact a solution of sorts is most often found by regulations fixing an upper limit for, say, the amount of noise legally emitted by planes, the amount of dust legally allowed in mines, the amount of smoke legally permitted from stacks, the amount of mercury legally released into a river.

Consider the "practical" difficulties if one were to determine how much the people living next to a noisy airport should receive from whom, or how much a mining company should pay to whom for a decrease in a miner's life expectancy by 12 years. The determination of these values would require very high transaction costs. The economic cost of getting the relevant information and the legal cost of getting all parties to agree would often surpass the amount of the damage. The transaction cost of telling your neighbor to keep his dog on his property, creating eternal animosity, far exceeds the possible gain of having a well-behaved neighbor.

As a matter of fact, many costs cannot even in principle be measured because of their highly subjective nature. Those living next to a smokestack could perhaps be refunded for their extra clothes-cleaning, house-painting and car-rusting expenses, and possibly also for their lung sickness, but not easily for the assault on their sense of beauty. Parents of thalidomide babies were haggling for more than a decade while the courts tried to play Solomon.

Economists who disregard such very real transaction costs put much too much stock in the suggested solution of internalizing externalities. Flat regulations can often be designed which are, at least, a stab in the right direction and which do not have high transaction costs.

Other Suggested Solutions

In theory, regulation is far from the best course of action. Its main advantage is that it is easy to understand and implement, although not always easy to police. Violators often get off with nominal fines in view of difficulties of proof and the white-collar nature of the crime. Polluters are innocent until proven guilty.

Cynics believe that they are less likely to be proven guilty the higher their station in life.

The problem with across-the-board regulations is that they do not leave free play to the marginality conditions. If two factories both pollute 1 ton of soot more than regulations permit, and one of them can clean up its extra ton of soot for $100 and the other for $500, then the regulation strikes uneven. Worse, it also strikes inefficiently, because the one factory might be able to clean up 10 tons of soot for the $500 it costs the other to get rid of 1 ton. This is clearly economically wasteful and socially harmful.

Such thoughts have led to proposals to tax pollution. Everybody would pollute up to the point where a marginal (extra) ton of pollution would cost more in taxes than internal clean-up would cost. Alternatively, pollution certificates could be issued and traded in the open market. If the total amount of pollution permitted by these certificates were less than the current amount of pollution, these certificates would be valuable, and the more valuable the greater the clean-up costs would be. In theory, this would be a very good solution, because it explicitly allows for marginality considerations and because the total amount of pollution can be easily controlled. Practical difficulties of defining, measuring, and comparing different sorts of pollutants, and of policing and enforcing, make this suggestion not universally attractive, but occasionally it will be far and away the best way out.

Throughout this discussion it should be kept in mind that the prevailing situation is often demonstrably deficient. A suggested solution need not be perfect to still be an improvement. "Optimizing" is a luxury for theoretical economists and mathematicians. Absence of an optimizing strategy is often an excuse for no action at all. A pitiable pitfall. A step in the right direction is better than no step at all.

7

Doomsday Predictions

Timing of Deaths

The increase in population and living standards, implying more production and consumption and thus more pollution and a faster depletion of natural resources, has generated a platoon of misfortunetellers armed with a large selection of doomsday predictions. In the most pessimistic versions, the human race will be completely wiped off the earth before long, leaving civilization—or what remains of it—to be dug up by evolutive-ant archeologists a billion years hence, much as we dig today for dinosaur bones from the Mesozoic era. It is somewhat ironic that these dinosaurs ruled supreme for over a hundred million years with brains not much larger than marbles.

In more palatable versions the population will be halved or decimated in some future decade, possibly the two-thousand-twenties, or -fifties. The survivors of the global disaster, the children and grandchildren of our present youngsters who weathered the holocaust, will continue to live on a much lower scale than today's, perhaps in a more or less static and stable equilibrium similar to that now prevailing in primitive areas.

Truly "optimistic doomers" may delay the decade of reckoning to the year 2100 or so. This would require a whole series of optimistic assumptions relating to technological development. In particular, a cheap, clean source of energy must become available, and the technology must be developed for harvesting the icecaps, the oceans, and the earth's core to deliver vast quantities of fresh water, minerals and food. Technology also must find a way to get rid of excess energy (heat).

Such assumptions may change the timing, but not the basic scenario. The crash, so long delayed, will be crushing when it finally arrives.

Choices of Deaths

The immediate causes of wholesale death differ from one doomsday vision to the next. They range from a rather straight-forward starving for lack of food or lack of resources to more fanciful suffocating in pollution much as fermenting yeast colonies are killed by their self-produced alcohol; or from exploding in global conflicts and international strife for space to esoteric roasting in self-generated heat; or from drowning as climate changes melt the icecaps to succumbing to epidemic deaths by strains of highly resistant cocci.

Large-scale disasters are not unknown to mankind. The Black Death which ravaged Europe in 1350 meant the abrupt end for roughly one in every four inhabitants. A gentler version of more recent vintage was Ireland's potato blight around 1850, sending

one in six prematurely to the grave, and twice that many to
greener pastures elsewhere, thus halving Ireland's population. (The
clear warning of the dangers of monocultures contained in this
example are rather nonchalantly disregarded by today's green
revolutionaries.)

Trivial by comparison is the 1970 drowning of half a million
or so would-be Bangladeshers in the brutal delta of what was East
Pakistan, or the deaths of unspecified numbers of Indochinese in
the bombings or on the battlefields of war. War, drowning, famine,
epidemics, take your pick. The four horsemen of the Apocalypse
would find themselves quite at home in the company of this
quartet.

Never mind differences in timing and methods, there is some
inexorable logic in these melodramatic predictions. It is certain,
however you slice it, that finite resources cannot support expanding populations and/or standards of living *ad infinitum*. If one tries
it anyway, the overtaxed system will inevitably break down. As
with all things cooking under pressure, the more time the heat has
to build up, the louder the explosion. The longer doomsday is
delayed, while populations continue to grow and living standards
rise, the more severe the doom will be.

Appraisal of Doomsday Scenarios

The logic of such apocalyptic views is impeccable. The relevance is more doubtful, especially the immediate relevance. A
number of factors tend to be dealt with in stepmotherly fashion.

First, there is the possibility that mankind may well react
adaptively or cybernetically, rather than purely automatically or
mechanically, to signals of impending doom, *provided the signals*

are clear enough. The argument goes that, as the crisis becomes more evident and the pinch is more acutely felt, mankind will more or less automatically adapt to a more sensible course of action, much as a driver avoids obstacles on the road. In this view, mankind will become more careful in using resources and energy, more deliberate in procreation.

This first line of defense is basically optimistic, claiming that in the end, collective reason will prevail. But histories of past civilizations which were totally obliterated for reasons solely stemming from within do not support too much optimism on this score. Mesopotamian rivers once made for lush valleys.

The second observation is that the future will have many surprises in store. Biochemistry is a science in its infancy, but it promises to stand a tall man. Physics and engineering have already mightily contributed, and continue to be astonishingly creative. Of the three factors of production—materials, energy, and information—the first may be finite and the second may be dwindling as a *cheap* resource, but the third is making up for it. Information grows and grows without depleting or polluting anything. Given some substitutability between these resources, pessimism is considered premature by those who buy this argument. Historically, they have a point.

The third argument is that while the physical limits of the globe are indisputable, and growth beyond bounds thus demonstrably impossible, these limits may well never be relevant because mankind has seen fit to resort to manmade devices to decimate the race. A shortage of domestic oil and unwillingness of others to provide the balance may well trigger a "quick and clean" demolition expedition.* Jealousy of the have-nots *vis-à-vis* the

---

*The premises of this remark hit closer to home today than at the time of writing in late 1972; the conclusion remains highly speculative.

haves could set off a nuclear venture. Even a bruised ego or childish temper tantrum may provide the motive for pushing the button.

Generally, human organization is apt to break up long before the physical limits are reached or exhausted. This is not always fully recognized. The unstable structure and divisive nature of our global society is certainly the most immediately relevant problem. It should be the concern of all. There is no reason to be overly concerned about drowning next year if you are going to be shot tomorrow.

Phrased more concretely, our concern should be to guide the system from one of destabilizing inequalities ("the rich get richer and the poor get children") to one of sustained, pleasantly and comfortably liveable, harmonious and balanced equilibrium for all. Such a prescription includes, therefore, an end to growth, but emphasizes that the distribution of whatever there is is an intrinsic part of the problem, and deserves priority.

The Basic Problem

The relevant question is whether we can guide the global system to some sort of stable state of population and environment —stable in the sense of enduring. If we wait for the holocaust, resources may be so depleted, the environment so polluted, and the human race—which has so magnificently adapted to the earth as it is but appears so little adaptable to major changes—so affected that earth will never again provide more than a handful of tribes the opportunity to eke out a meager existence. This would be an enduring equilibrium, but an unfortunate one.

8

Pipeline, Threshold, and Trigger

Where We Are

Mastering Mount Everest in the fifties, manning the moon in the sixties, or diving and delving to record depths in the seventies are all spectacular successes. In all these instances, however, the *structure* of the problem is essentially trivial: you know where you are and you know where you want to go. The problem itself, *how* to get there, may be exceedingly difficult or even impossible, but that is another matter.

The challenge to guiding world development on a course to enduring and agreeable equilibrium is complicated by the fact that we do not quite know where we are at present, and have only the vaguest notion about where we want to go, or even what the alternative options are.

We do not quite know where we are: the globe's current population and population composition, the exact amount of reserves of resources, the present state of air, water, solid waste, noise, heat, and radiation pollution are all unknown. Moreover, even in principle many of these quantities are extremely difficult to define and measure, and they interact in complex, synergistic ways.

The Pipeline

The real difficulty, however, is more worrisome: we do not quite know to what and to what extent we are irrevocably committed. The DDT sprayed in the sixties in Surinam will, during the seventies, be a building block for babies in Bali when, via the rivers and the oceans and the plankton and the fish and the chickens the humans consume it in concentrated dosages, and the mothers' milk dispenses it willy-nilly. Turn and twist as we might, the sequence is inevitable, although the long delays, the many links, and the wide distances involved make it less visible. The largely beneficial, short-run, local effect of DDT is vastly different from its largely detrimental, long-run, global effect.

Such long-delayed consequences are often called *pipeline* effects. The name is well-chosen. In taking a shower the temperature of the water in the pipe between the faucet and the showerhead *can no further be influenced*, never mind how one tunes, turns and twists the knobs. No current action can change the temperature, whether ice-cold or scalding hot, of the water in that pipe. One is as helpless as the driver of a skidding car, unable to avoid a clearly visible mishap.

In a similar vein, it is not without relevance that in many nations, particularly in South America, 20 percent to 25 percent of the populations are females below 16 years of age. Barring just a few, 15 years from today all these girls will be fertile. Fifteen years later again, they will still all be fertile. Even if, in such a country, a law were enacted today and scrupulously enforced allowing at most two children per family, the population would continue to increase until around the year 2035. A pipeline effect.

The pipeline holds what will inevitably come out, but not necessarily tomorrow. The *lead time* is the time which must inevitably pass before the pipeline begins to flow. There is a 15-year lead time before girl-babies become potential mothers. There may be a 3-second lead time before a skidding car hits an abutment. There is a substantial but somewhat vague lead time before we can generate sufficient energy from sources other than fossil fuels.

A Detour on Feedback Loops and Ecosystems

The DDT chain, showing how Surinam spraying is linked to Balinese babies, seems too fanciful and flippant to be taken seriously. That would be a mistake. The construction of such chains is the basic task of all science, whether history or biology or whatever.

Some chains are cycles. Such a cycle always begins and ends with the same commodity, and is called a feedback loop in engineering parlance. The importance of feedback loops is that they can pinpoint with some accuracy which situations are explosive and thus carry the seeds of their own destruction, and which are stable or in search of equilibrium.

A simple example of a feedback loop is: *more* people get *more* babies which gives *more* people. This situation is potentially explosive, for there is nothing in the mechanism to ever stop more people from becoming even more. By contrast, the loop *excess* demand gives *higher* prices which leads to *lower* demand is in principle stable. In this case, demand cannot grow forever, for resulting higher prices would curtail demand. The plight of public transport can be summarized in a nutshell by the loop *fewer* passengers means *smaller* frequency which leads to *fewer* passengers still. Such loops are often called vicious circles, but they are more aptly described as vicious spirals.

It is an interesting parlor game, though hardly hard science, to conjure up such cycles of causes and consequences. One feedback loop proves that the number of old maids is essentially stable—it cannot grow forever. The "proof": *More* old maids will have *more* cats which eat *more* mice and thus leave *less* food for skunks and thereby *fewer* predators for bees and thus *better* pollination of plants leading to *better* animal fodder and *better* beef, which makes for *more* virile males and hence *fewer* old maids.

Unfortunately, a similar tortuous route proves the opposite. The "proof": *More* old maids have *more* cats who eat *more* fish which requires *more* fishermen which implies as a statistical certainty *more* drowned fishermen and hence even *more* old maids.

The scientific problem is to identify the dominant effects, and to determine the lags and other reaction parameters of the system. Even then the task is not finished. Constant monitoring is required, for such chains and loops are not eternal fixtures ordained by Allah or Zeus—they will change with the passage of time, or, indeed, by human interference.

This is particularly evident in the feedback loops that occur in nature, the so-called ecosystems. An ecosystem describes who eats what and is eaten by whom. Stability in ecosystems largely depends on complexity. If many animals prey on many others and are, in turn, preyed upon by many others, a sudden drop in number of one particular species will not disturb the basic stability. For the animals that used to eat the species in short supply have sufficiently many substitutes for dinner so as to prevent their demise, and the animals that used to be eaten by that species have sufficiently many predators left so as to prevent their uninhibited multiplication. But simpler systems are potentially very unstable. If mice were the only ant-eaters, and if owls were to eat exclusively mice, then the killing of mice by men would spell the end of the owl, and a prolific increase of ants. Men, with his inimitable ability to interfere with the cycles of nature, has often simplified an ecosystem in precisely such a way, wittingly or inadvertently. Monocultures developed from a few strains of highly productive crops similarly introduce uniformity and simplicity that invite disaster. So does incest: lack of variability in the genes of the sex partners greatly increases the probability of defective offspring.

The Threshold

The twin of the pipeline effect is the threshold effect. The *threshold* value is the point at which a stimulus is of sufficient intensity to begin to produce an effect. In practice this value is often only vaguely known. At what concentration does DDT begin to have a perceptible effect on health, lifetime, offspring, eyesight, or whatever? At what increase in global temperature will the icecaps begin to melt, at what decrease will Boston become polar?

Even when knowledge about instantaneous thresholds is exact (99 percent of all eggs will crack when dropped on stone from a height of two centimeters) knowledge about the thresholds of persistent and possibly cumulative stimuli is virtually totally lacking. There is no measurable or perceptible influence of having 200 parts per million DDT in your fat for one day. But what about having only 20 parts per million DDT in your body, cozily lodging in your fat day after day after day? DDT is very persistent (it decays very slowly) and the effects may accumulate over time. Similarly, one hot day in the arctic will not bother the Dutch dikes, but no one knows how many fingers would be needed for those dikes if the arctic temperature were higher by 5 degrees for a century. A persistent drip can destroy a rock.

The Trigger

Pipeline and threshold together form a perilous pair, for once we observe that the danger threshold has been passed, the pipeline will—come hell or high water—expose us to further doses, possibly sufficient to literally produce hell or high water.

The *trigger* effect is often the sister of the twins: a very small quantity can trigger a very large event. A little more water in the reservoir can trigger a respectable earthquake. A little more sewage in the river can dramatically affect its self-cleaning powers. A few more cars on the road can greatly increase the congestion. In all these cases, all goes well up to a point. Beyond that point, often referred to as the critical point or critical mass, nothing goes well. Plants do perfectly well in cold nights, as long as the temperature does not drop below 33 degrees Fahrenheit. Below 32 degrees they die very fast. A large change from 100 to 33 degrees is taken in stride. A small change from 33 degrees to 31 degrees is promptly lethal.

Presence of a trigger means that the range of tolerance between a noticeable effect and a deadly end is small.

The Family of Three

The family of pipeline, threshold, and trigger is a truly dangerous family. It is conceivable that all of us are already doomed to die as thresholds (which keep us blissfully ignorant of any impending danger since the effects of that danger are not yet noticeable) and pipelines (which force us to swallow more of the dangerous stuff even when it is fully recognized as harmful) and triggers (the small tolerances above thresholds) combine to seal our fate. The carbon dioxide in the air, plus what will unavoidably be added because it is in the pipeline, may prevent the earth's heat from being radiated back into space, leaving mankind as well as all of the animal kingdom slowly simmering, shishkebabbed on sunrays. Or, more likely, a substantial increase in genetic defects of future generations may already be wholly unavoidable.

To a great extent, therefore, the future is mortgaged by the present. In many instances, at an *unknown* rate of interest. The cigarette smoker in the thirties, forties, and fifties was happily unaware of the price he was to pay decades later. The car driver is largely unaware of the cumulative consequences of exhausting more and more carbon and nitrogen oxides into the atmosphere. Worse than that, even the scientists do not really know. We do not quite know where we stand, and we may not find out until doomsday is in the pipeline.

9

Democratic Decisions

Democracy

We may not know exactly where we stand, and the precise amount of the final billing for our "pollute now—pay later" philosophy. But we surely do not know where to go. Some vociferously advocate zero population growth, others hold such a position to be immoral. Some indignantly proclaim any pollution too much pollution, others would rather have some smokestacks huffing and puffing away than unemployed husbands puffing and huffing at home. Some favor depletion allowances for extracting irreplaceable resources, others argue that such activities should be surtaxed. Most are woefully unconcerned and blissfully ignorant about all of these issues.

It is not obvious how these conflicting views will be resolved. It is obvious, however, that they will, or ought to be, resolved in a democratic framework. Democracy is the type of rule in which the government is the servant and not the master of the people, in which the government exists for the benefit of those who create and support it, in which the government is responsive to the will of the people, or in which . . . fill in your own nice sounding phrase in this general vein. On paper it looks magnificent. In reality, any democratic government has at least three built-in, structural flaws, quite apart from the fact that there is a noticeable discrepancy between the lofty ideals of "servant, not master," or "responsive to the will of the people," and the day-to-day practice.

Timing of Decisions

The first weakness is that democratic decisions are not likely to be timely decisions. They are occasionally made fast, without thinking through the consequences or the alternatives, as a result of acute public pressure, a passing fad, or, most likely, an upcoming election. In Medicare legislation, or automobile exhaust legislation, as some examples of many, time and thought are needed to assess the short-run and long-run effects of the decisions and to study the repercussions of the decisions outside their intended area, and the interaction with decisions made elsewhere, and the economic cost-benefit analyses in comparison with alternative options, over and above the time and thought needed to get the basic facts and data straight. The presently enacted laws in these areas display some signs of unwarranted speed.

More characteristically, however, the mills of democratic government, with all its checks and balances, grind slowly, if indeed they grind at all. Decisions are often unconscionably long delayed, or even are watered down into that most perverse of all decisions, no decision at all. Quite typically, the delay between societal action (or sorts) and the recognition of a serious problem takes decades, whether it concerns the dangers of smoking, DDT, pollution, population levels and growth, auto safety, or scarcity of energy and resources.

The crunch must be felt acutely before painful rules and regulations, such as rationing gas, are politically viable. Before that time, problems are relegated to innumerable committees of experts and bureaucrats. The ostensible task of these committees is to produce a report recommending some specific action, or at the very least some specific alternative actions. The actual reason for the committees is to condone delay while creating the impression of concern. The very composition of the committees—the experts who are politically naive and are concerned with proving one another wrong, and the civil servants who are loath to rock the boat and are jockeying for position in the lineup—acts as a nearly insurmountable impediment to the recommending of any action whatever. Mundane platitudes are what the executive really wants and what the committee can freely give. A committee report is valued the higher the less practical consequence it has. Obviously, when action is finally taken it bears little relation to any report. The ritual dance of committees is an exercise in futility indispensible in any democracy, for it legitimatizes delay.

Fortunately, vastly improved communication and media coverage has recently speeded up the action somewhat. The dangers of delay, however, remain, and are far from hypothetical. A wise proposal of lowering taxes to stimulate a sluggish economy may be poor policy when finally enacted in a different phase of the cycle.

Shelving Democratic Niceties

More importantly, in matters of life and death, when time is of the essence and the choice becomes more poignant—"Is it better to go democratically down the drain together, or to somehow survive?"—it can easily be defended that the democratic niceties should be shelved temporarily. "Democracy is not worth much when we are all dead" is a more compelling argument than the thought that life is not worth living without democratic freedoms. The courage of those willing to die for such abstract principles— and history is replete with examples—is respected and applauded. Even in dying for a wrong cause or when in vain there is the value of preserving one's dignity and integrity. But the saving grace of such actions should be the implied "I die so that you may live better."

The major problem is that some emergencies are not easily recognized as such. Population and pollution problems, which frequently are characterized by short triggers, high thresholds, and long pipelines, may give rise to a situation where the democratic majority, or even the government itself, is totally unaware that it is speeding toward a deep abyss. Under such circumstances a strong autocratic driver should *perhaps* take charge. It would be better by far to educate the voters of the speed and direction of such problems so that they might democratically arrive at timely corrective actions.

Short Horizon

A second weakness of the democratic process is that frequent elections lead to a short horizon for most political decisions. During his short term a President or Prime Minister may well be able to cope with a 5-percent, or even a 10-percent rise in population, or a consistent balance of payments deficit, or a persistent rate of inflation. If the crunch will be felt only later, unpopular corrective actions will probably be delayed. Few democratically elected leaders with an instinct for self-survival can afford to make decisions which are painful in the short run and beneficial in the long run, if they have the option to make decisions which are painless for the time being. Never mind the malefic long-run consequences. (The choice between currently painful but eventually beneficial action and current inaction leading to long-run problems is not confined to governments. The decision to abort or not has a strikingly similar structure.)

Thus, in democracies we tend to get short-run answers to long-run problems, if these problems are considered at all. Politicians are tacticians and not strategists. Such short-run answers often aggravate the long-run problem. A basic balance of payments disequilibrium that can currently be solved by a mildly painful adjustment in the rate of exchange carries the seeds of a future, excruciatingly painful upheaval of major dimensions.

The oft-suggested redesign of the democratic process, including elections for longer terms (a 7-year switch?) with no, or at lower levels perhaps one, consecutive reelection, would help politicians a long way towards a more long-run vision of their responsibilities. The suggestion is not without merit, but not without drawbacks, either: for reasons hard to fathom, political leaders occasionally indulge in truly perverse actions, with malefic short-run consequences not offset by any reasonable hope of beneficial long-run effects. Vietnam is a case in point. The corrective medicine for such stupidities is to throw the ruling party out of office. This medicine works slowly, and would be slower still if terms of office were for longer durations.

A less debatable and more important step forward could be

made by committing budgets for long-haul projects on a long-run basis. The yearly recurring budget debates frustrate any attempt toward decent long-run planning.

Pressure Groups

A third problem of democracies is the power of pressure groups. Any organization having an ax to grind, and some resources to lobby or bribe with, can exert a power far greater than its numbers warrant. In the United States one can think of GM and IT&T, or the Sierra Club and the Audubon Society, or labor unions and consumer unions, or Planned Parenthood and Zero Population Growth, or Black Power and Women's Lib, or the Catholic Church and Common Cause.

Often it is all to the good that a vocal, concerned, committed group attempts to speed reforms, regulations, and rules they feel are needed, even if they form but a minuscule proportion of the electorate. In many cases, however, the pressure group is shamelessly selfish in its objectives, and can achieve success only because the "victims" of their proposals are widely spread and only marginally affected—not enough to make it worth anyone's while to exert counterpressure. This is why many pollution regulations are lax and permissive, why strip mining concessions are liberally granted, and why ineffective and expensive drugs are aggressively marketed—all are examples of pointed industry lobbying versus diffuse damage. In a similar vein, the National Rifle Association has been instrumental in guaranteeing that guns remain staple items in American homes. Guns give rather pointed damage, of course, but the *probability* of being so damaged is diffuse.

If not shamelessly selfish, the pressure group is often curiously one-sided and absolutist. It is tempting, sitting before an open fire and sipping a second martini, to get very exercised about the DDT-induced plight of the peregrine falcon. DDT, however, does more than produce wafer-thin eggshells—it also protects millions from malaria. There is a trade-off here, and it should be faced squarely. Even in sober thought one might well conclude that the demise of a species is more serious than premature death for millions of people. But it is not obvious. There is something unwholesome about being liberal with other people's children or other people's money. The nagging doubt is not easily dispelled that if *your* children or *your* money were at stake the vision would be more perceptive. In the new perspective the falcon might not loom quite as large, the deaths not quite as remote.

Autocracy

Democracies tend to react slowly, they tend to have short-run vision, and they tend to be vulnerable to pressure groups and bribe-brokers. Enlightened autocracy would clearly be better, but democratic rule is to be preferred because a ruthless autocracy can be infinitely worse than even a badly functioning democratic framework, and because in the nature of autocracy there is no mechanism to prevent an enlightened one from becoming a despotic one. The prime advantage of democracy is not that it is so good, but that when it is bad it is still much better than the excesses to which any other alternative so easily, indeed nearly inevitably, leads. It is best in a minimax sense.

Errors of Commission

Whatever the form of government, a vexing problem is to determine the limits of legitimate governmental intervention in the individual's life, liberty, and pursuit of happiness. What are the limits of power society can exercise over the individual?

It is fruitful to answer this question by considering the purpose of governmental interference. If this purpose is to prevent harm to others—that is, unpleasant externalities of your actions for others—then interference is appropriate, in principle. The specific mode of interference or the specific shape of the stipulation is, of course, open to debate.

A host of actions with pronounced externalities are regulated for this very good reason. They range from prohibition to power-mow lawns on Sunday morning, to obligations to be inocculated, to dress codes prohibiting indecent exposure or public nudity. Laws prohibiting child labor and minimum schooling laws can be defended by the same principle. There would be innumerable unpleasant externalities for all if half the population could not read or write.

Sometimes, unfortunately, individual actions with no visible externalities are regulated. Blue laws prohibiting sale of alcohol on Sunday fall in this area. So do laws forbidding homosexual acts and abortion. Such activities, discreetly performed by consenting adults, are without significant externalities, and society should stop playing guardian angel over the morals, beliefs, and tastes of others, however peculiar these morals, beliefs, and tastes may be. Not only society, but individuals also should stop playing moralistic games of one-upmanship.

Detour on Abortion

The issue of abortion in particular is too hotly contested and too close to population problems to let it go in passing. There is, on this issue, no need to work oneself up into a frenzy of holier-than-thouism. There should be no dispute that more careful and controlled behavior at the *moment suprême* would have been vastly preferable, even at the cost of making that *moment* a little less *suprême*.

The moralizing is unwarranted, however. It is not so very moral to beget a baby that is at best unwanted, and at worst unprovided for with love, food, and education; or, to the extent that it is so provided only at the cost of other needy being further deprived. It is a trade-off between bads, a doomed-if-you-do, doomed-if-you-don't situation singularly ill-suited for jeering from the sidelines. Jeering which adds a guilt to the already severely taxed emotions of the hapless mother is particularly offensive. Jeering by males is particularly incongruent.

Even those holding life sacred in an absolute and uncompromising way should recognize that, quintessentially, the choice may well be between one person living 70 years at subsistence, and two persons living 30 years under submarginal conditions, for a net gain of 10 years and a lot less misery. A similar choice is frequently made in a more evident and immediate framework when it is a matter of mother or child.

Morality is a function of the state of the system; it is no absolute magnitude, it has no sense in a vacuum. No lesser a mind than Socrates was all gung-ho for infanticide *à la Sparta*, where a newborn baby was submerged for some prolonged period to test whether he was fit enough to withstand the rigors of this baptism. Too bad if he was not. In certain tribes in Tibet polyandric practices are accompanied by physical elimination of most baby-girls, measures deemed essential for tribal survival in these bleak regions.

"Fanny Dooley loves humanity but hates people" is an improper conjunction in this day and age. It should read: "Fanny Dooley loves humanity and therefore hates people". In most parts of the globe that is the only version that makes sense.

True freedom surely contains as a most essential element the freedom to change, the flexibility to reconsider. A fixed and immutable position is no freedom. It is dogma.

Errors of Omission

Even as the Government sometimes errs by commission, as when it regulates actions without externalities, so it sometimes errs by omission, as when it fails to regulate actions with manifold externalities. Sometimes this is simply a temporary shortcoming, for it is difficult to quickly adapt the laws to fast-changing circumstances. The snowmobile craze with all its obnoxious externalities may have caught many lawmakers temporarily off-guard.

Sometimes the error is more structural. The most noteworthy example is bedroom creativity. Such creativity creates many spill-overs prejudicial to the interests of others. That is precisely the condition which sets the stage for governmental interference with the liberty of its members. Just as it is legitimate to legislate against drunken driving with its horrible spillover effects but unwarranted to call for prohibition, so it is unwarranted to regulate intercourse (or more deviant or imaginative sexual artistry), but it is well within the legitimate domain of governmental concern to regulate the consequences of intercourse with their multifaceted externalities.

10

Where to Go

On Maxima

"Where to go" should not be dictated by scientists, however wise, or religious leaders, however holy, or any particular country, however powerful. It should instead be based on a majority consensus distilled by some form of democratic process.

It is not implied that scientists should be silent. Theirs is the task to spell out in some detail the range of feasible options. Religious and political leaders may then help shape the actual choice by whatever scripture they propound or rhetoric they command.

Perhaps the most pressing and relevant question to be answered in order to determine our objective is: "What is the maximum number of people the globe can support at a given standard of living, for an indefinite period of time?" Or, alternatively "What is the maximum standard of living that can be maintained for a given number of people?"

The answer is that for any given number of people the achievable and maintainable living standard will in large measure depend on advances in cheap and clean energy supply, ocean and earth's-core harvesting techniques, and agricultural and technological progress, the latter area including improved pollution-control devices, recycling techniques and procedures, and transportation and distribution methods. It is challenging to speculate on these issues, and to determine for various sets of assumptions regarding these matters the maximum level that can be supported *in perpetuum* for any given number. Conversely, one might attempt to assess the maximum number of people that can be accommodated at any given standard of living.

Why Maxima?

On second thought, however, no basic human value is served by aiming for those maxima which strain the world's capacity to absorb punishment to the limit. For one thing, it is risky, because a faulty assumption or wrong calculation may result in overshooting the feasible equilibrium, requiring a painful contraction later. (The maximum criminal penalty, death, is risky for much the same reason. Posthumous rehabilitation falls short of adequate remedy.)

Quite apart from such risks, the fact that ten people *could* be supported at a given level does not mean that ten people *should* be supported; one may be content with eight. The two so excluded from dinner on earth cannot conceivably have any objection to this arrangement, since they do not exist. No argument is more void of reason than the one that we owe something to a nonexisting entity, or better, nonexisting nonentity. By contrast, we owe at least a moral debt to those who do exist, for the mere fact of having invited them.

We do not always pay this debt. The poor nations often default. Less excusably, in wealthy economies many lose out in the shuffle of the stacked deck. Rich nations are also poor in preventing "statistical" deaths—the highway divider is not built even though, as a matter of statistical certainty, three persons are bound to die as a result of this neglect. As long as these persons are no more identified than the winning tickets in a lottery before the draw, society is willing to live with it, hiding behind (at best) a cost-benefit analysis and (at worst) governmental nonchalance. This is in stark contrast with the virtually unlimited amount of money and effort expended to save an identified person. Our lack of concern for the statistical deaths of the living gives an embarrassingly hollow ring to our professed concern for the lives of those unborn and even unborne.

Population Size

While the choice of population size will be inversely related to the standard of living, these two quantities need not be jointly determined. It is perfectly legitimate to determine in principle only the population size, and to leave the standard of living somewhat vague, more or less depending upon the precise speed and nature of technical progress and societal development.

Regarding this choice of population size, many reputable scientists believe that the current population is already too large, in relation to the technical competence and resources available, to be afforded a modicum of decent life. The pipeline will further increase population at a rate outstripping anticipated technological advances and resource development. In this view, the relevant problem is how to put fast and effective, yet reasonable and decent, brakes on population growth.

Other reputable scientists assess the evidence differently. They believe that 10 or even 20 billion people could be sufficiently, though somewhat Spartanly, supported at equilibrium. Even if true this is small solace, for on the one hand there is no intrinsic value in attaining such maximum feasible values, and on the other hand it would only delay (and with time aggravate) the problem of control. The delay would be less than a century if current growth rates persist.

Optimum Population Size

It is only fair to confess quite emphatically that, at a given technology and for a given area, the problem of determining the "optimum" population has not been solved. It depends on many factors, including the distribution of the population over the area. Population and pollution have in common that a substantial part of the troubles they create is due to their very uneven distribution. We do know that there is a population value so low that more are welcome, and a value so high that more are detrimental, and a probably wide stretch in-between which is perfectly serviceable and close to optimal. We also know that this range of near-optimality is often overshot.

At first, the benefits of growth outweigh the costs. More people can share the indivisible costs of roads, schools, and churches. More people create diversity and choice of movies, lifestyles, and jobs. More people will result in a more efficient division of labor.

Eventually, the costs of growth outweigh the benefits. Every single chimney pollutes increasingly many, and there are increasingly many chimneys. The choice of movies is no longer confined to a handful of happily perspicuous options, but overwhelms one with an acute sense of frustration. The labor force is so large and each job so specific that it takes an ever-growing army to merely coordinate the efforts.

Yet growth continues. This is partly due to the inertia of the system, the mere momentum of growth itself. Partly it is due to the fact that individual decisions pertaining to offspring are not subservient to the general interest. And partly it comes about because the power-structure continues to profit from, and hence continues to actively promote, growth—although the general population no longer benefits. This is true whether the power is political, or based on money, or vested in the hierarchy of the church.

Population Too Large?

Most of us are not scientists. But even for laymen the handwriting on the wall ought to be pretty clear. For the many people who are destitute, the question is not how well they live, the wonder is that they live at all. For the many poor the daily problem of feeding many mouths is a recurrent and abhorrent reminder of numbers too large. But even for those who are well-off, not all is wine and roses. For far too many of us, far too many of our daily frustrations and anxieties result from not being able to do, or the mere fear of not being able to do, what one wants to do because of "all the others." In the United States, fear of a filled parking lot makes one gobble up a hasty breakfast; fingers dance on the telephone dial forever in search of a free line; flights are booked weeks in advance; queues and waiting times are long.

It is true, of course, that a good deal of that fleeting, "ah,-things-go-well" feeling is due to the pleasure of finding a parking place, the delight of getting a telephone connection, and the happiness of acquiring a flight ticket on the spur of the moment. The reflective mind is apt to ponder, however, to what level of depravation, degradation, indeed, degeneration we have come by the force of sheer numbers, when so important a daily slice of happiness is merely the absence of misery. For the hunters of the Stone Age who successfully axed an ox, happiness must have been a more exhilarating and rewarding experience. Today's artificially generated thrills, canoeing a rocky river or skiing a steep slope, or the passive entertainment provided by football gladiators or Ann and Abby, are poor substitutes.

The Siamese twins of relativity, space and time, are the only truly scarce resources even for the rich, and they will become more so when increasing numbers encroach on space and induce wasted waiting time. Privacy will be threatened and property rights infringed upon as massive numbers force private affairs to become public property (it is hard to hide your snoring in a duplex), and private property a public affair (it is tough to be forbidden to play *your* transistor radio on the beach).

Design of Control Mechanism

No one, whether convinced of the urgency of the problem of numbers or inclined to view it only as a potential problem for the distant future, can reasonably disagree with the proposition that it would be eminently useful to design a workable population control mechanism, which, if needed, could be called into action to curb growth beyond a certain number, or to allow growth only in a controlled manner. The controls could be relaxed as technological breakthroughs allow for quantum steps forward—such as when the sun can be tapped for energy, or the ocean and icecaps milked for water, food, and minerals, or the earth's core opened up for energy and minerals. The controls could be loosened a bit when fusion energy proves safe and feasible, or green revolutions become greener still. The controls can be manipulated as limits grow and constraints fade. But mainly, *the controls can be controlled.*

This is the key problem, and we will focus on it more closely after a short detour discussing some well-known but nonetheless important issues relating to the standard of living.

11

Standard of Living

Per Capita Gross National Product

The standard of living in a country is conventionally determined by a deceptively simple and simply deceptive statistic, the *per capita gross national product, pcGNP*. This statistic is determined by dividing the market value of the yearly output—be it tomatoes or shoes, face-lifts or fishhooks—by the total number of people.

Shortcomings of GNP

The measure defies common sense in at least three respects as a result of the concept of *market* value.

1. If a housewife makes the beds, cooks the meals, mows the lawn, or repairs a sock, she does not add to the national product. A chambermaid, a cook, a gardener, and a seamstress do.

The absence of a monetary payoff for a housewife's services leaves it unregistered by GNP-measuring seismographs. Two hundred million beds made each day, at 2 minutes a bed and "wages" of $2 per hour would add $10 billion to the yearly GNP.

2. The productive output of those who provide services is measured by their salaries, for lack of anything better. These, after all, are recorded by the market mechanism. The result is that the values of teachers, barbers, civil servants, police, doctors, reverends, etc., are determined by their wages, although highly paid police need not be more effective in curtailing crime, well-paid teachers do not necessarily teach better or more, prosperous preachers do not preach more inspirational sermons, and a haircut is a haircut is a haircut, whether it costs $3, $1, or a dime. This anomaly extends beyond the service sector: a $15,000 car does not necessarily provide better transportation than a $2,000 car, although it may have more sex- or snob-appeal.

3. There are no deductions for unwanted goods (bads) that do not pass through the market, such as exhausts produced by a car or generator. Indeed, not only is the negative output not deducted to get some measure of the real contribution to welfare, but the required clean-up costs are *added* as contributions to the GNP, as when smoke-damaged lungs need doctor's attention. The national product might be $1,000 higher by having a car accident and spending $400 to repair the metal mess and $600 to landscape your nose again than if there were no accident in the first place.

A further shortcoming of the GNP is that it adds with equal equanimity the market value of goods and necessities and those of bads and wastes. A man who lives 60 miles from his work generously contributes to the GNP with his wasteful commuting costs. A nation half on tranquillizers and half on stimulants has on both scores a higher GNP than one of healthy and happy, sound and sane, supple and subtle bodies and minds.

Alternative Welfare Index

The pcGNP measure of the standard of living leaves a lot to be desired. Its shortcomings easily lead to distorted impressions. Although it may be true that the American pcGNP is roughly 20 times the Tunisian pcGNP, it is an unwarranted conclusion that the average American lives 20 times better than the average Tunisian.

A more viable statistic of the standard of living would be a *welfare index*, a single value derived from a composite function including variables such as life expectancy, the percentage literacy at age 12, the average duration of education, the average consumption of calories, proteins, and vitamins, the average population density and degree of urbanization, the standard amount of free time, the percentage of income allocated to the 20 percent worst off in the population, the average number of sick mandays per year, the levels of air and water pollution—as well as some variables pertaining to material well-being, such as the average number of rooms per person, the percentage of families owning at least one bath, TV, radio, refrigerator, car, etc.

Such a function is not currently defined, nor will its value be easy to measure, if indeed that is feasible at all. It is sobering to reflect, however, that despite the fast growth of GNP in the developed nations during the sixties, none of the nonmaterial ingredients of welfare improved markedly, and many deteriorated noticeably.

Critique of Welfare Indices

Even the very complex index suggested above is not really good enough. It does not, for example, incorporate the number of manhours spent coding computer cards or picking California grapes. There are many such mind-dulling, back-breaking jobs with every ounce of the nobility of labor squeezed out, every element of pride in accomplishment eliminated. Spending a lifetime chiseling at a pillar in some cathedral cannot have been much fun either, but somehow seems more rewarding. If we want to measure general welfare, a miserable job ought to be one component. Another component not mentioned is "freedom;" for example, freedom of press or freedom to have as many children as one wants. Undeniably, these are important aspects of welfare. Undeniably, they cannot be measured or properly assessed. Nor can the fear of being mugged by gangsters or bugged by the Government be properly incorporated, even though it cannot but decrease welfare if one doesn't dare to walk in the streets, or talk on the telephone.

All of this, however, is sniping from the sidelines. The real problem is far more basic. "General welfare" may well be an untenable concept. The reason is that many specific or particular welfares, presumably collectively making the general welfare, are at loggerheads with each other. Just as one may be happier with $10,000 if the neighbor makes only $9,000 than with $12,000 if the neighbor makes $15,000, so society at large must recognize that it is often not the absolute level of well-being, but the relative level, that counts. It is not the size of the pie as measured by GNP or otherwise, but the distribution of the pie that is relevant in determining the general perception of welfare. It is in production that labor and capital are complements; in distribution, they are competitors. It is around the Christmas tree that grandparents, parents, and children sing carols together; the rest of the year the interests of the old, the employed, and the young are at variance.

In Defense of GNP

So where do we stand? On the one hand we have a carefully defined, accurately measured, and widely used GNP and pcGNP. Despite shortcomings, it is quite useful as long as it is used for comparisons between similar countries or to measure changes between not too distant years. As with all index numbers, the level is hard to appraise, but changes from year to year or comparisons across countries are far less tenuous, because, whatever defects there are, they are shared consistently by all measurements. Comparisons between the 1890 GNP and the 1980 GNP, or between American GNP and Tunesian GNP are less appropriate, but also less useful.

On the other hand, we can construct an alternative general welfare index, redefined to take "negatives" such as pollution into account, and purported to measure Net Economic Welfare instead of Gross National Product. The initials now spell the appropriate acronym NEW. NEW measures clearly have advantages from a theoretical point of view, but from a practical point of view they may be premature. The reason for this is that for the vast majority of people, including 80 percent of all U.S. citizens, the foremost ingredient of welfare is all that money can buy—call it material well-being. Worry about pollution is a luxury for the affluent; the vast majority worries about shoes for their children. The GNP, with its emphasis on market values, may thus be more relevant—for the time being.

pcGNP Values

The pcGNP does, especially in the lower ranges, give a rough and ready impression of a country's general well-being, or lack of it. Close to the bottom of the rankings we find India, Indonesia, and Kenya with a pcGNP of around $100. For Brazil, Ghana, and Taiwan the value is around $250. The overall world figure is $600, and the United States tops the list with about $4,000. The global pie is rather unevenly divided, with obscene riches side by side with obscene poverty.

There is, of course, no consensus as to what constitutes an equitable distribution of income on a global scale. Indeed, there is no consensus on a national scale, where, *typically*, the richest 5 percent share 20 percent of the total output, and the poorest 20 percent share 5 percent, and where, *sporadically*, the richest 5 percent share 60 percent of the total output, and the poorest 20 percent share 2 percent. Wide agreement, at least in the abstract, will be found for the proposition that it ought to be more equal than it is. This would not only help to assuage an outraged sense of decency, but, more importantly, help create conditions more favorable to economic growth and development. Extreme inequalities do generate large savings by the rich, but these savings are not used to invest in factories making pots and pans or shirts and slacks —who would be around to buy these? They are used instead to buy land and luxury yachts fabricated in some foreign country. A country's prosperity not only depends on a reliable supply of savings provided by the rich, but equally on a solid source of demand provided by the masses. Gainfully employed shoemakers buying bread from happily productive bakers are more important than a few rich buying an occasional cake or an odd pair of alligator-hide shoes.

(In)equality between Countries

To achieve more equality *between* countries, fairly sizeable transfers from the prosperous to the poor nations on a sustained basis are needed. These contributions should give the rich countries some leverage in the attempt to solicit cooperation from the poor countries on population control. There is, admittedly, something vaguely immoral about trying to coax a consensus with coins. In this particular instance, however, the approach has merit and even morals.

For one thing, the poor countries currently have by far the greatest population growth rate and population pipeline, so that they must change their habits the most to get growth under control. For another, the rich nations have much more reason to share their fortunes once they can be assured that not all progress will be siphoned away by larger populations.

But there is more to it than that. The rich countries pollute the air and the water at rates orders of magnitude larger than the poor ones, yet the very mobility of air and water makes pollutees of rich and poor alike. The rich export a sizeable part of their pollution, and it is only fair that they should pay for the damaging externalities thus imposed on others. Furthermore, they exhaust the resources and exploit the whales and the offshore oil fields, to the detriment of all, including future generations.

Finally, the rich have more to lose than the poor from cataclysmic events, and so there is ample reason for the rich countries to pay the poor countries as added inducement to control population growth. To prevent overtones of paternalism the prosperous countries should, of course, put their own house in order as well.

(In)equality within Countries

What is true *between* countries is largely true *within* countries. The exception is that in most countries it is *not* systematically true that the poor are more reproductive than the rich. There is no pronounced correlation between wealth and number of offspring; the very poor and the very rich display some tendency to have more children than the very middle class.

But it is *still* true that the rich pollute much more than the poor. The poor, often secluded and largely separate in the self-perpetuating poverty cultures of urban ghettos and the rural slums of inaccessible villages do not perceptibly pollute the rich. The rich, using lots of electricity, driving lots of cars, and controlling all productive processes pollute the poor by making trashcans of oceans and atmosphere. The rich, by being rich and inevitably displaying it, perhaps even flaunting it, make the poor realize they are poor: a particularly vicious externality. Without the rich being rich the poor would not be poor. The poor do not usurp resources; the rich do. The rich do not compensate the poor for all or any of the spillover effects thus imposed.

The "We-Can-Afford-It" Syndrome

To put it another way, it is a stubborn fallacy to believe that having children is all right as long as one cay pay for them. In truth, one *cannot* pay for them. Who compensates the rest of mankind for all of us having a little less space, having to wait a little longer, having the environment a little more polluted and resources a little more depleted? Not the parents. They pay for food and shelter and some amenities, but they do not compensate anyone for all the externalities. Nor—and this is the crux—*could* they do so even if they *wanted* to: there is no market for transfer payments to indemnify others for externalities. The presence of vast externalities has destroyed the workings of the price mechanism, with all its automatic controls and signals, information and incentives. No one can be said, truly and fairly, to pay for his own child; least of all, paradoxically, can the rich make this claim, for they generate the spillovers. Even in death they consume space galore.

The "but-we-can-afford-it" syndrome appears reasonable until one stops to think that we (that is, all of us) cannot really afford it (that is, all of them). The follow-up argument, that as long as your children can reasonably be expected to become doctors rather than garbage collectors they ought to be welcome, is also quite fallacious. There is not one iota of evidence that doctors are worth more over and above what they earn than garbage collectors.

There is always the hope of siring a second Shakespeare, of course, but realization of such a wish appears to be a largely random event. Many of the greatest minds came from the humblest origins. Erasmus was the son of a priest and a prostitute. A man unparalleled in fame was the son of a poor carpenter.

12

Six Methods

Do Nothing and Moral Suasion

The most compelling conclusion so far is that a mechanism must be designed to enable control of population growth. In the long run, if breeding goes unchecked, mass starvation or collective suffocation or mushroom clouds or whatever will lead to wholesale deaths, and thus a "natural" check on uninhibited growth. To prevent such traumatic experiences deliberate checks must be designed and implemented when needed.

Whenever there is too much of something (people, pollution, corn), or not enough of something (parking space, soldiers, energy) the government has six ways to react.

1. The government can *do nothing* and hope that market forces or perhaps a miracle will solve the problem. This will typically be the prime strategy when there is a shortage of housing in some suburb, a balance of payments deficit in some quarter, or a large inventory of unsold automobiles on May 31. This strategy

is also used when all parties agree something ought to be done, but nobody knows precisely what, or when no agreement can be reached. The trivial truth that no action is also an action is often conveniently ignored.

2. The government can resort to *moral suasion* and exhortation; it can point to the national interest, exult about the rewards of being a good citizen, and induce guilt feelings for noncompliance. This approach is used to sell U.S. savings bonds, to limit the use of water in summer months, or to recycle paper.

Investments, Regulations, Charges, Subsidies

3. The government can *invest* to alleviate the shortage or get rid of the surplus. Thus, it can build more parking spaces, it can buy up surplus agricultural commodities or give export subsidies for them, or it can pay higher wages to increase the number of volunteer soldiers.

4. The government can *regulate*. It can ration food in short supply, it can enact military service laws, it can establish the maximum noise level a motorcycle can legally emit. In extreme but in no way exceptional cases the regulation takes the form of *prohibition*. It can prohibit the burning of autumn leaves or the planting of corn. Often the regulations come in the form of *commands*. One must be vaccinated and one must shovel one's sidewalk.

5. The government can *charge* for the use of scarce products, such as charges for parking spaces and for access to a national park. It can also charge for creating surpluses, such as the charge for sewage and garbage disposal or for dumping industrial waste.

6. It can *subsidize* for not using scarce resources, as when it

subsidizes public transportation; or for not creating surpluses, as when it pays farmers for *not* planting corn.

These six methods are obviously not mutually exclusive. Seldom is one method used in isolation. To get more soldiers the government may well resort to moral suasion (your country needs YOU!) *and* subsidies ($1,500 if you sign on the dotted line) *and* investments (in higher pay scales) *and* regulation (service laws). The six methods are, however, collectively exhaustive; there are no other methods of control.

Do Nothing and Moral Suasion to Control Population

One or a mixture of these six methods will have to be used to curb population growth, lest it be curbed, drastically and dramatically, by some horrifying disaster. We will consider the merits of the methods, in turn.

1. The time-honored method of doing nothing is unlikely to be effective. It is true that, in general, the population growth declines the more developed the country is, but this effect is neither pronounced enough (even the most prosperous countries have a positive growth rate) nor fast enough (living standards go up very slowly if at all in many underdeveloped countries). It is true that, with delays, birth rates adapt to death rates, but not enough to stop growth. Doing nothing is an ostrich-like policy in the face of clear danger, and likely to be suicidal.

2. Moral suasion is a welcome, if immoral, instrument. Those who restrict the number of their children by taking the advice of Zero Population Growth or the condoms of Planned Parenthood are helping those who do not, so that "virtue" gets punished and "vice" rewarded. This immoral side effect is always generated by

the instrument of moral suasion, and makes it unattractive and ineffective in the long run. Moral suasion works best for small numbers for short durations in the face of compelling arguments. Population is a case of many numbers, long durations, and complex arguments. It would be eminently useful, however, if moral suasion could sway the view of the Pope and other influential wielders of dogmatic barriers.

In China moral suasion, aided by a large dose of patriotism and peer pressure, has been quite effective in limiting population growth. The pressures were so immense, however (including public confessions of sins and massive ridicule) that they would be regarded as intolerable infringements on freedom elsewhere. It is a moot point whether the Chinese method can still be referred to as moral suasion. Some would call it a club-in-the-closet method.

Investments, Regulations, and Charges to Control Population

3. The strategy of *investment* tackles the symptoms but worsens the disease. To try to diminish the unpleasant side effects of population growth by investing billions upon billions in infrastructure and houses has been the predominant approach in the past. It has effectively delayed recognition of the seriousness of the problem and aggravated our present plight. One particular investment, however, that of freely dispensing birth-control advice and devices, is quite helpful.

4. *Regulation* has not often been seriously considered, partly because of so-called principles involved (the privacy of the bedroom doctrine) and partly because of pragmatic enforcement problems. Yet, society enforces monogamy, one husband per wife and vice versa, even when this violates religious principles or hedonistic

philosophies. Society could similarly decree that no woman may bear more than two children, or something to that effect. More sensible and flexible regulations can be conjured up. Policing and enforcement of such rules must be considered in detail. The principle of regulation cannot be discarded out of hand.

5. *Charges*, or fines, for having children are somewhat inequitable and not likely to be very helpful. They are inequitable because they would blatantly favor the rich, who are precisely the main culprits where pollution and depletion are concerned. Two hundred million Americans are far more taxing to the world than 800 million Chinese. Charges would not be very helpful, since about 60 percent of the world population could not pay the charges.

Subsidies for Population Control

6. By contrast, subsidies for *not* having children seem feasible. It is flippant to even jocularly suggest that the U.S. Government give a 25-inch color TV to every woman who allows herself to be sterilized without having any children, a 15-inch color TV to a woman with one child, and a mini black-and-white for those having two. It would, however, be cheap for society, a definite bargain compared with schooling costs alone.

Subsidies have an element of bribery which is unwholesome. A subsidy can be viewed as a negative charge, and while charges are bad because 60 percent cannot pay them, subsidies are bad because 60 percent are greatly tempted to fall for them. This creates an asymmetry, which is inevitable when one set of regulations covers a broad spectrum of different situations. In this instance, the asymmetry is particularly suspect, for it cannot help but foster the impression that the rich are after the birthrights of the poor.

Far from giving subsidies for *not* having children, society at present subsidizes *having* children by its tax regulations, free schooling, and so on. The wisdom of these laws, often enacted in the belief that larger numbers further the glory of nation and God, should be reconsidered. The balance between private and public costs of having children should perhaps be somewhat restored. Some externalities should perhaps be internalized.

The operative word in these sentences is *perhaps*. The case is not obvious. Once children are born, it is in the interest of society that they be well-fed and well-schooled. Poor feeding not only hampers physical health, it also impairs mental health and intelligence. Poor schooling is wasteful of human capital and detrimental to the joy of living. To do away with tax concessions and demand payment for schooling will unquestionably affect poor children in ways which would create their own costly externalities on society— the poor would remain physically unfit and mentally untrained.

So here is the dilemma: internalizing externalities will lead to fewer (poor) children, but those that are born anyway will be the prime victims, and society at large will later be a secondary victim. What we really want is fewer children, but all of them able to achieve their full potential. Once again, across-the-board regulations for widely divergent circumstances are not satisfactory. This is also true, of course, of the present tax regulations and free schooling laws. They are not ideal, either.

13

Population Control

Regulation and Limitation

The interpretation of the word "control" in population control is ambivalent. It can be interpreted as in cost control, where it essentially means limitation. It can be interpreted as in temperature control, where it essentially means regulation. It is population regulation we are interested in, not necessarily limitation. The emphasis on limitation is exclusively a function of current historical relevance. As we continue to discuss population control we will mean regulation, but in many examples we will focus on limitation. Population control as a concept is neither for nor against life, neither for nor against growth, but simply for an ability to regulate if the alternative is unregulated disaster.

Use of Control Mechanism

The design of a population control mechanism does not necessarily imply its use, now or ever, any more than the acquisition of a fire extinguisher implies use. It is a precaution, to be used as the situation warrants. And it is for the government to determine when this will be the case and how it will be used.

This is not simply an idle disclaimer. Population growth is quite cyclical, especially in developed countries. It changes with the political and economic climate, or with a change in the inheritance laws. In the United States births have been as low as 14, and as high as 26 per thousand per year since the Second World War. At present it is at an all-time low, fluctuating around and occasionally dipping below replacement level.

In England the birth and death trends from 1920 to 1940 were such that, had they been maintained, Englands 2040 population would have been 10 percent of its 1940 population. In the late thirties 100 British women produced an average of 85 girls during their lifetime of fertility. Some serious concern about the vanishing British race prevailed, not unlike the present concern for overpopulation, and likewise largely based on the fallacy of extrapolating trends. In our present concern we may be chasing a phantom ghost, or fighting a dragon without fire, especially in the case of *some* countries or regions. It is by no means precluded that past patterns will change in the face of a crisis or for a host of other reasons, or even for no demonstrable reason at all.

Fear of Population Decrease

The concern of the British for the number of British roaming their isle is quite typical. For somewhat obscure reasons, each nation considers any decline in numbers, or even a potential future decline in numbers, with grave concern. It is apparently axiomatic for any given nation that fewer of its nationals would be a severe blow to its international prestige and pecking order, if not, oh *hubris*! to mankind.

This vision does not extend beyond borders. No one outside Holland seems to feel that what this world needs is more Dutchmen barricaded behind dikes and Deltaplans at a density of a thousand per square mile. The Dutch, meanwhile, happily continue to add Protestants to their Protestants and Catholics to their Catholics, as if survival of their race or religion were in doubt. In autarky no more than 2 million Dutch could be supported by their polders and windmills.

Let us change the scene to Rumania. In 1962 the Rumanian birthrate had dropped below replacement level to about 13 or 14 per thousand. To be sure, in view of the pipeline, the Rumanian population still increased, but at the prevailing birthrate it would have begun to decline around the year 2010. The Rumanian government was concerned at first, then alarmed. Late in 1966, to buck the trend, they suddenly and summarily *il*legalized abortions, which used to be the main method of birth control practiced, and which were safe, secret, without social stigma, and cheap—one abortion for the price of eight condoms.

As a result, the birthrate soared. By the autumn of 1967, a scant seven months later, the birthrate had tripled to 39 or 40 per thousand. Today, the women (and men) have adapted to the new rules of the game by adopting a different game plan. The birthrate once again is below 20 per thousand. Meanwhile, the 1967-1968 cohort of babies will reverberate through the Rumanian system for the next century. The first wave of babies clogging their schools at present will create a second wave around 1990, and so on. Production of baby food has become quite cyclical in Rumania, but that is the least of the problems created by such violent swings in fertility. In its concern for the survival of Rumanians, the Government panicked half a century before growth would have stopped.

Fear of declining, or level, populations is sometimes motivated by a belief that population growth is necessary for economic growth. This is a wholly unwarranted belief, without even a shadow of likelihood. Economic growth is a function of technological advance and higher investments per worker—both epitomized by the use of computers instead of feather pens in bookkeeping. The of necessity gradual move toward a stable population will lead to a more rectangular—instead of broad-based triangular—population pyramid, implying fewer dependents per family, higher savings, more investment per worker, and fewer people with more to spend rather than more people with less. There will obviously have to be shifts in the aggregate consumption basket as the age distribution changes and more money becomes available per household. To some extent, quality will replace quantity, and vacations will replace diapers. Such gradual changes could be taken in stride by planned and capitalistic economies alike. In fact, far more sudden and drastic changes—the overnight obsolescence of electric desk calculators, for example—have been absorbed by the system without much of a ripple, and traumatic energy shortages, while sending shockwaves throughout the system and crippling some established patterns of behavior, serve to speed up technological breakthroughs rather than to stunt growth.

Other Population Problems

Population growth or cyclical swings in population growth are only a few of the population problems. The uneven distribution of population, leading to urbanization and crowding, is another problem. Such problems are of a different scope altogether, and will not be discussed beyond the observation that at a certain point the critical mass is reached where the critical space a person needs is insufficient. At that point, civility breaks down. Crowding is not an experience that elevates one's mind. Extreme crowding degrades.

Other demographic problems, such as a lack of virile males in some populations due to war, or a population "pyramid" with an hourglass shape, are also beyond our scope. Such problems, however, could be mitigated and even prevented in future eras by the use of a proper regulation mechanism.

Externalities of Control Design

Even if never used, the design of a more deliberate control mechanism is no luxury. If need be, it can and should be used as a prevention against doomsday disasters when the globe is visibly about to give up its ghost. It might also be used to great advantage in preventing violent swings in fertility.

Beyond those obvious uses, there is also the option of using it to allow trade-offs between fewer people at a higher standard of living, or more at lower. Individual families routinely choose between a car or a baby.

Moreover, its effects are not exclusively regulatory. There could, if the mechanism were properly designed, be positive spillover effects, such as a more egalitarian distribution of wealth and income, a greater sense of cohesiveness of the different nations encompassing the globe when, by working together, they break the exponential growth barrier, or greater sense of appreciation for the younger generations as their numbers dwindle and they become "scarce," or even simply a realization and awareness on the part of prospective parents of the seriousness of their decision.

For all these reasons, then, the design of a control mechanism is no luxury.

It is to such a design that we can turn. In Chapter 14 we give a national control proposal, which is further illustrated in Chapter 15 and criticized in Chapter 16. In Chapter 17 we present a global control proposal. In Chapter 18 we integrate the global with the national proposals.

14

National Population Control

Three Criteria

In principle, the plan designed here is not meant for any one country in particular; it may be useful, however, to keep in the back of one's mind the idea of a developed country with severe population problems and a mature social conscience and a well-run bureaucracy. The Netherlands would fit this description.

A plan for effective offspring regulation ought to meet three criteria, in the following order of importance:

1. It ought to be politically acceptable, or at least have a fighting chance of being accepted.
2. It ought to be organizationally, economically, and medically feasible to implement.
3. It ought to recognize and permit diversity in attitudes and circumstances.

To be politically acceptable, it is essential that the need for some form of formal regulation is recognized, and that the particular regulation proposed be convincingly fair. To guarantee feasible implementation, the regulations ought to be simple to understand and routine to police. To allow for diversity, the regulations ought to leave freedom for individual choice.

A Straw Man Proposal

The concrete and simple proposal to give every woman the right to bear two, but no more than two, children does not measure up too well against these criteria. On the plus side, it is brutally easy to implement, the brutal part being forced sterilization after two children. On the minus side, such a sweeping proposal, while seemingly egalitarian and fair, is neither in a world of our diversity. Equal is not fair and fair is not equal. It makes no sense to impose the same rigid constraints on all women, whether nun or farmer's wife, whether having a pronounced mother-urge or none, whether rich or poor. A solid minus should also be chalked up for political acceptability. The *vox populi* would resoundingly defeat it, for there is little tangible benefit to be gained by anyone and the thought that *your* third child would harm the chances for survival of the human race is too far-fetched to be taken seriously.

Some of these registered shortcomings could be mitigated by the introduction of a market in certificates for children, with every woman beginning with two such certificates. In particular, this would give different women with different desires for children a chance to express their feelings by buying or selling certificates. However, if the unfettered law of demand and supply were operative, the rich would face a largely ineffective constraint. The rich are precisely the worst polluters and usurpers of scarce resources. Politically, such a market would be doomed at its dawn, because the poor would rightly view it with great suspicion, and there are many poor.

Enough. Enough about all such straw man proposals put up to blow them down with the next breath. It is time to spell out a specific and workable, fair and flexible system. Here it is.

Certificates

Certificates. Every woman, at age 15, is given two certificates *in her name*, each of which is good for the birth of one child. At age 30, she can sell the certificate to the national control agency. This agency, in turn, will sell certificates in the name of those who want to buy.

Comment. In principle, it is also possible to give one certificate to each youngster, male or female, at age 15. In the interest of symmetry this might be preferable. It is also possible to give 2.3 or 1.9 certificates, in which case the agency ought to buy or sell fractional certificates. This creates no problem. The requirement that the certificates can be sold only at age 30 or later is designed to prevent the unthinking young from exchanging future potential children for ready hard cash. For administrative reasons certificates could have a maximum lifetime or expiration date, such as 35 years after date of issue. Note in particular that, whether selling or buying certificates, one can only deal with the agency, and that all certificates are in name (or in social security number!)

Multiples

Multiples. A multiple is established for each couple or each single girl wanting to sell or buy certificates. This multiple simply gives the *ratio* between buying and selling price for that couple. If a couple has a multiple of 5, this would imply that it would cost that couple 5 times as much to buy a certificate as it would get for selling a certificate.

Comment. This multiple need only be established if a transaction is contemplated. For each couple, the multiple is an increasing function of its prosperity. It should be a simple function with few ingredients: the current capital (assets minus debts) of the couple, its current income, its expected income stream, and its expected inheritances. Its computation is worth further scrutiny, which is delayed to the next chapter. Here it suffices to establish the principle. No couple would have a multiple less than 1, and no multiple would be higher than a specified maximum, perhaps 20 but possibly 100. To fix ideas, in a population of 1,000 couples there might be 100-1s, 250-2s, 200-3s, 100-4s and 350 with multiples over 4, including perhaps 17 couples with a multiple of 9 and one with a multiple of 60.

Prices

Prices. The price p at which the national agency will buy certificates from couples (and therefore the price at which couples can sell to the agency) is a linearly increasing function of the multiple m of the couple selling, $p = a + bm$. In this equation, a is the intercept and b is the slope coefficient. The value of b must be positive. A couple with multiple m can thus sell its certificate for a price $p = a + bm$; but if it wants to buy a certificate from the agency it will have to pay a price $pm = (a + bm)m$, as indicated in the previous section.

Comment. One could take any type of increasing function, but a linear one is simple enough to be easily comprehensible, and its *two* parameters, known as intercept and slope, not only allow for some flexibility in use, but also allow for the possibility to meet *two* objectives.

For example, it could be that the agency establishes a price function $p = \$(50 + 50m)$. Such a function would imply that a couple with multiple 1 can sell its certificate to the agency for $100, and a couple with multiple 9 can *sell* a certificate for $500. This last couple would, however, have to pay 9 × $500 = $4,500 if it wanted to *buy* a certificate from the agency, so that a high multiple is quite decidedly a mixed blessing. The couple with multiple 1 can buy for the same price it sells, that is, $100.

The agency's price function could also be $p = \$(100m)$ or $p = \$(20 + 80m)$. In both these cases the family with multiple 1 will still get only $100 for a certificate it sells, or pay $100 for an extra certificate it buys. The family with multiple 9 will now get $900 or $740 for a certificate it *sells*. The price at which these families can now *buy* a certificate has risen from 9 × ($500) = $4,500 to 9 × ($900) = $8,100 or 9 × ($740) = $6,660, respectively. Thus we incorporate, via these concepts of multiplier and price function, the idea that rich children are more demanding of the environment and more malicious in their externalities than poor ones.

By changing the price function, the total number of certificates can be controlled. This can and usually will be one of the two objectives the mechanism can accommodate. If, with the price function $p = \$(50 + 50m)$ more certificates are bought from the agency than sold to the agency, and if this is against the policies of the government which wishes to stabilize population growth, then it is a simple matter to change the function to $\$(50 + 70m)$, say. This would make the price at which the agency buys higher and the price at which it sells also higher. Thus, couples would find it more attractive to sell, and more expensive to buy, certificates.

Initially a certain amount of experimentation may be needed to find equilibrium or desired values, but later fairly few and fairly small changes should suffice to guide the controls in desired ways.

Profits

Profits. The market system is obviously profitable provided that multiples are not less than 1 and that approximately the same number of certificates is bought and sold. The profit should, among other things, be used to defray the administrative costs of running the agency.

Comment. We refer to what follows, and in particular to the numerical examples in the next chapter, for further details.

Problems

Problems. The problems can be roughly grouped into five categories. In order of increasing importance these are:

problems of detail, problems of pricing, psychological problems, medical and ethical problems, and problems of
(political) acceptability.

Comment. Problems of *detail* include such issues as what
to do about multiple births, with women or children who die, with
adoption, and so on. Sensible and reasonable answers to these
problems are not difficult to construct. One could rule that a
multiple birth counts for 1, that a dead woman's ticket is part of
her estate (but can only be sold to the agency since the certificate is in her name), that a woman gets a new certificate for free
when her child dies before age 21, provided she is still fertile, etc.
Adoption rules need some more specific detail to cover the large
variety of different cases, but it can be done routinely. As a
general rule, the one who gets the child should give up a certificate,
and the biological mother giving up her child should get her
certificate, relinquished at birth, back.

Problems of *pricing* include the difficulty of keeping price
fluctuations limited, and questions as to what price shall prevail for
transactions. It is suggested that the latter question be answered by
the price function prevailing at the date the multiple is determined.

Psychological problems are more difficult. For example,
women quite content to be childless now might get the urge to
procreate because children are rationed. Rationing can create its
own demand, and to the extent that it does the proposal is
counterproductive in limiting population. Also, children rather
than jewels or jet-set vacations might become hallmarks of riches
and affluence, showpieces of ostentatious consumption, sources of
vicious envy. This last problem can, perhaps, be somewhat mitigated by forbidding more than four children to anyone.

More Serious Problems

A serious set of problems is *ethical* and *medical* in nature: What to do with women who have, by giving birth or selling certificates, none left? The suggestion is, nothing. But what then if they give birth again and cannot acquire another certificate? This is an extraordinarily sensitive point, only relevant to the poor. The nonpoor can always acquire another certificate. One might suggest, not wholly in jest, that the poor couple incurs a debt to society equal to the price of what a certificate would have cost, and that further procreation be prevented by sterilization. Neither part of this "solution" is attractive. To force the very poor to pay only makes them poorer still and is very bad for the other members of the family. To force sterilization has very ominous overtones of castrating the poor. This is clearly an issue deserving a more detailed and incisive answer. It will be given in Chapter 16.

In the meantime, we take solace in the fact that the agency might be able to prevent too many of such situations by using part of its profits to stimulate voluntary sterilization or, preferably, to hand out to the poor (that is, those with low multiples) free birth-control devices covering the whole spectrum from rhythm rosaries to abortion services upon request. Now that we have largely conquered the tyranny over the minds of men, it is high time to end the tyranny over the bodies of women.

Problems of *political acceptability* are severe. Regulation where freedom prevailed before starts with many strikes against it. Also, there seems little to be gained for any one country to curtail its population growth if the rest of mankind unabashedly proceeds with the process of transforming this garden of delight into a lunar landscape. Even if implemented in isolation by an individual country, however, it would have equitable effects in forcing the rich to pay sizeable sums for aggressive procreation and in inducing the poor not to have too many children.

Actually, under the proposal a woman of age 15 gets something which will be of market value later (two certificates), as well as the certainty that her children will find space left to play and frolic, live and learn, not to mention breathe and drink. The price she pays is the knowledge that any number of children over two will cost her extra money, although not more than she can afford. For about 50 percent of the women this is no constraint at all: they do not or would not have more than two children anyway.

If well presented and vividly and convincingly documented and publicized, the scheme appears a candidate for a majority of votes, especially as time proceeds and minds ripen, and the fear of the poor can be shown to be, if not wholly illusory, at least balanced by benefits. Without regulation the current "freedom" to procreate may prove as illusory as the freedom to use the commons. Paradoxically, regulation can increase freedom. Freedom is much greater for the regulation that we can only drive on the right side of the road.

15

Sample Computations

Determination of the Multiple

The determination of the multiple for the ith family, m_i, is unnecessary unless the ith family wants to sell or buy a certificate. At that time, the multiple will be determined with the help of some tables and schedules, not unlike taxtables but less complicated.

The value m_i will be a function of the general well-being of the family. This general well-being is relevant, because it determines on the one hand the ability to pay, and on the other hand the affluence with which the offspring will be surrounded and therefore the externalities it will generate. As a rough-and-ready guideline, a family will spend 2½ times its yearly income on raising a child from birth through high school—his food and fees, shoes and shots, room and rides. The more affluent, the more electric guitars will be played in backyard suburban garages, scattering externalities North and South and East and West.

The general well-being is not solely determined by the current situation, that is, the current yearly income and the current net worth. It should also incorporate reasonable expectations pertaining to future incomes and inheritances.

The current income, whenever it is worth mentioning, is available for income tax purposes anyway. It may be hard to determine to the nearest penny, but it is certainly known within what range it falls.

The net worth is simply the difference between assets and liabilities. It may be difficult to determine to the dollar, but in the vast majority of cases it will be possible to quickly determine whether it is below $5,000 or above, whether it is between $75,000 and $100,000 or not.

The expected lifetime income stream is quite relevant for student-couples, for example. Their assets may be negative, and their income nonexistent, but a doctor-to-be can expect to earn quite a good living as time goes on, and even his third child will lack for little. For the sake of simplicity, it can be roughly defined as the norm for the profession. Once again, within very broad ranges these can be estimated.

As for anticipated inheritances, a rough-and-ready computation of the parents' net worth divided by the number of their offspring can readily be made. In all those computations interest, discounting, current values, and changes through time of the capital can be disregarded, because it is the ranking and not the absolute value that will be relevant. The result may be somewhat arbitrary, but it will not be quixotic. It will also be easy to determine. A couple whose wife's parents are worth $20,000 to be divided over four children, and whose husband's parents have $200,000 to be split in three, has a value of about $72,000 for anticipated inheritances. In appropriate cases other relatives should be similarly considered. Rich relatives sometimes share their bounty before they die, and grandparents might even give the young couple a certificate for the third child. Their wealth should certainly be a factor.

Points for Components of Well-Being

For each of these components, points are scored, much as a bank scores points in credit applications. A sample illustration may be useful, and is given in the first table.

Current net worth of couple (thousands)	*Points*	*Current income of couple (thousands)*	*Points*	*Antic. lifet. inc. stream (thousands)*	*Points*	*Antic. inher. of couple (thousands)*	*Points*
⩽ 5	0	⩽ 5	0	⩽ 200	0	⩽ 20	0
10	1	7	1	300	1	30	1
15	2	9	3	400	2	40	2
20	3	11	5	500	4	50	3
30	5	15	10	600	6	75	6
40	7	20	17	700	8	100	9
50	10	30	25	800	10	200	12
75	15	40	35	900	12	300	15
100	20	60	45	1,000	15	400	18
500	30	100	55	1,500	20	500	21
⩽1,000	40	⩽200	65	⩽2,000	30	⩽1,000	25
>1,000	50	>200	75	>2,000	40	>1,000	35

The point scores can be argued forever and a day. The fact that they are there is more important than what they are precisely.

In assessing the merits of these figures it is not so much their absolute level as their relative comparison that should be looked at. For example, a family with net worth of $50,000 and a yearly income of $11,000 is viewed as roughly equivalent to a family whose net worth is only $30,000, but whose yearly income is $15,000.

Conversion of Points into Multiples

The next table presents the conversion of points into multiples. This conversion might be as follows.

Points	*Multiple*	*Points*	*Multiple*
0- 2	1	51- 60	12
3- 5	2	61- 70	14
6- 7	3	71- 80	16
8- 9	4	81- 90	18
10-11	5	91-100	20
12-15	6	101-110	25
16-20	7	111-120	30
21-30	8	121-140	40
31-40	9	141-170	55
41-50	10	171-200	70

The Price Function

Suppose next that the price function is $\$(50 + 100m)$, implying that a couple with multiple 8 can sell their certificate for

$850, but needs 8 X $850 = $6,800 to buy a certificate from the national agency. That couple has somewhere between 20 and 30 points, and typically might have $18,000 in capital (net worth) for 3 points, $14,000 current yearly income for 10 points, $900,000 expected lifetime earnings for 12 points, and $40,000 in future inheritances for 2 points. Surely such a family can afford $6,800, and surely their child will be going through life crying in bankteller queues, leaving tricycles unattended on the sidewalk overnight, punching your Katy on the nose with his toy gun, kicking baseballs in your rose-gardens, and, in general, liberally dispensing externalities all over the place. To put the amount in further perspective, the family will spend around $35,000 on the upbringing of this child.

A truly rich family, with capital in excess of $1 million, annual income of over $500,000, expected lifetime earnings well in excess of $2 million, and more than $1 million to be inherited, such a rich family would need to pay 70 X $7,050 = $493,500 for the privilege of having a third child. This is a lot of money, but it is less than their yearly income and probably much less than half of the family's current capital. The child will later own acres and acres of real estate off-limits to trespassers—which would comprise virtually all the rest of mankind.

Profit for Agency

In further sample computations, for illustrative purposes only, we can summarize the action at the national agency for one day.

Couple with multiple	Wanting to sell	At a price of	Wanting to buy	At a price of	Net for agency	
1	17	150	13	150	-	600
2	14	250	8	500	+	500
3	8	350	9	1,050	+	6,650
4	4	450	5	1,800	+	7,200
5	1	550	2	2,750	+	4,950
6	2	650	4	3,900	+	14,300
7	3	750	1	5,250	+	3,000
8	1	850	1	6,800	+	5,950
9	-	950	4	8,550	+	34,200
10	-	1,050	-	10,500		-
12	1	1,250	-	15,000	-	1,250
14	2	1,450	1	20,300	+	17,400
16	-	1,650	1	26,400	+	26,400
25	1	2,550	-	63,750	-	2,550
					+	116,150

The prices at which the agency buys certificates are given by $(50 + 100m)$ as before. A couple with multiple 8 will receive $850 for its ticket. For couples wanting to buy the price is determined by multiplying their multiple with their selling price, e.g., $8 \times \$850 = \$6,800$ for couples with multiple 8. The agency ends up with a net of $116,150, which funds can be used to pay for administrative expenses and to supply birth-control advice, devices and services. The agency can "play" with its price function if too many couples sell their certificates by lowering the function to $(50 + 70m)$ or so. In the converse case, it should up the ante.

Mathematical Summary

The multiple m_i of the *i*th family is a function of four variables, net worth, current yearly income, expected lifetime income and anticipated inheritances. If we write w, x, y, z for those factors we have

$$m_i = f(w, x, y, z).$$

Moreover, $f(0, 0, 0, 0) = 1$ and $f(\infty, \infty, \infty, \infty) =$ some finite integer value, 70 when using our tables. Finally, for whatever values of w, x, y, and z, the value of m_i will be an integer.

A family *i* with multiple m_i will receive an amount

$$\$(a + bm_i)$$

for selling its certificate to the agency, and it will have to pay

$$\$(a + bm_i)m_i$$

for buying a certificate from the agency.

If p_m stands for the number of families with multiple m who buy a certificate from the agency during some year, and q_m for the number of families with multiple m who sell a certificate to the agency during that year, then the agency has a net of

$$\$\left[\sum_m (p_m m - q_m)(a + bm) \right]$$

If p_m and q_m are roughly comparable for all *m*-values, and b is not too small, this will be a nice kitty.

16

The Case Against

Against the Poor

When the preceding proposal was introduced at seminars, a number of objections were raised repeatedly against a background noise of sniggers and giggles, chuckles and chortles of general disbelief. By far the most common argument was that, however you slice it, the plan is against the poor. "Somehow the poor will be screwed again" is the vulgar formulation of this critique in a nutshell. A carrot means more for a hungry man that caviar for a rich man, so $100 can easily bribe a poor man, but $1,000 will leave a rich man unmoved. Moreover, the frightening spectacle of forced sterilization, however jocularly raised, will only pertain to the poor.

The answer that it is not the intention, or the inevitable consequence, of the proposal to eliminate procreation by the poor is not remotely good enough. The case is far too sensitive and emotionally loaded to be put to rest with good intentions.

The answer which *is* good enough argues that the *two* parameters *a* and *b* of the price function allow one to meet *two* criteria. One of these criteria will nearly always be to achieve a desired growth rate, possibly a zero growth rate. This may require some trial-and-error, some tinkering and experimentation, but there are no basic problems.

The second objective could be that there should *also* be a zero growth rate for the poor, that is, those with multiple 1, or multiples 1 and 2 combined. One may find that the price function $(20 + 180m)$ will equate overall demand for and supply of certificates, and thus result in a zero growth rate. It may well be, however, that with this price function far more poor people sell their certificates for $200 than buy a certificate for $200, an amount they simply do not have. Some poor cannot go bankrupt for lack of the $50 registration fee.

On the other hand, the function $(-200 + 250m)$ may also equate overall demand and supply, and moreover, result in about the same number of very low multiple families buying and selling certificates for $50. It is by this mechanism that the proposal can explicitly guarantee that the poor will not be disenfranchised in the market for children.

Sterilization

While it can thus be guaranteed that at least in the aggregate the poor will not be deprived of children, they can still be sterilized. If a poor family has a third child without having, or being able to acquire, a certificate, it was suggested that they be sterilized. In practice this will probably mean the woman, but it is reasonable to suggest that the husband might be sterilized instead, at the couple's choice.

Forced sterilization smacks too much of the infamous *Endlösung* to be tolerable. It tampers too much with ingrained values of decency, although, of course, it is not the sterilization that is necessarily bad, but the forcible aspect of it. Forced abortion would be equally repulsive. The fact that the operation would be safely, freely, and discreetly performed would not make this forcible aspect any better. It would make the operation much more appealing to those who freely choose to be sterilized, and it might induce some to so choose, but not all would opt freely for this alternative, however attractively packaged.

There are various ways out. One is to establish a price function such that the poorest class—those with multiple 1—is not effectively in the market. By making the slope coefficient b equal to minus the intercept a, as in the price function $\$(-100 + 100m)$, those with multiple 1 never have to pay for certificates, nor will they receive any money for certificates. Since anyone with a multiple in excess of 1 should be able to pay, the problem of sterilization would become moot.

This is attractive, but there are disadvantages to the suggestion. For one, imposing $b = -a$ takes away one of the two parameters and thus one can no longer satisfy two criteria. For another, if the very poor are essentially out of the market they can "freely" procreate, but still without the money to raise their offspring. Moreover, while the poor do not create many obnoxious externalities for the rich over and beyond an occasional short pang of conscience, they do create many "internal externalities" within their own family. The presence of a third or fourth child is not going to help the first child get any better shoes or food or space in bedrooms. Furthermore, to leave one group essentially out of the market may in and of itself reinforce the social stigma of "we-don't-belong," a feeling so often recorded by welfare recipients.

It seems better to use the parameters of the price function to equate overall demand and supply as well as the demand and supply of the poor. It can then happen that a couple with multiple 1 has a third child without certificate or any chance of buying one for $50. The suggestion is to allow this without any penalties, no fine, no debt, no need to buy a certificate, no sterilization—for families with multiple 1, to be sure. If, however, they beget a fourth child and therefore a second child without certificate, then either husband or wife should be sterilized.

All previous comments and objections against forced sterilization remain valid. But society has an obligation *vis-à-vis* itself, and *vis-à-vis* the offspring already present, which at some point should prevail over the rights, however basic, of the parents. By allowing one child of grace, so to speak, the occurrence of involuntary sterilization will be less frequent, but it will not be wholly absent. It is never pleasant to compromise principles, but never to compromise can lead to ludicrous situations.

Poor and Rich Nations

Another criticism, and one with substantial merit, questions which nations are going to adopt this proposal, and the reasons they would have for doing so. The two main comments in this vein are "The rich nations don't need it, and the poor nations cannot afford it" and "The nation that adopts it is really a sucker, for others will continue to pollute and deplete while they behave themselves."

There is a grain of truth in the comment that the rich do not need it and the poor cannot afford it. The rich countries by and large have shown declining birthrates, and a few more scary headlines or further liberalization of birth-control measures or changes in tax allowance or child support laws may be sufficient to achieve zero growth. In the United States in some recent months birth levels have been below replacement rates, and while this is scant evidence of having licked the exponential growth curve once and for all, it is a welcome change.

"The poor countries cannot afford it" summarizes concisely that, for many underdeveloped countries, the organizational effort, bureaucratic infrastructure, and medical services required just cannot be mustered. This is a valid observation, to which we will return in the next chapter on the global population control proposal.

The more nearly correct aphorism, however, is: "The poor nations absolutely must control their populations as a prerequisite for economic growth, and the rich nations must control it because of their much too exponential economic growth." If the rich see fit to keep population in line without formal regulation, then that is perhaps so much the better, but it is a shaky foundation to build on. The more successful "unregulated" control is, the less the reason for keeping it up. The regulation mechanism need not be used, but its presence and potential use can only have a stabilizing influence on erratic cyclical behavior and unwanted growth behavior.

The idea that vice gets rewarded and virtue punished when one nation adopts the proposal also has merit. In the extreme case where only one nation does not adopt the proposal while all others do, that one nation profits greatly by being less polluted and having longer lasting global resources, and all the while doing what comes naturally. There is thus no reason at all for anyone to adopt the plan. National chauvinism will make it very hard to sell to any one nation. It will prove impossible to explain to Turkish peasants or Brazilian fishermen or Dutch farmers that regulation is required if Greece, Argentine, and Belgium get along without. All this is also a powerful argument for tackling the problem on a more global scale.

The concept of a nation is a little old-fashioned and out-moded anyway in this day of jet travel, many interactions and interdependencies, and nuclear devices and communication satel-lites wholly immune to national borders. That these communica-tion channels hardly help nations to communicate beyond major sporting events or a royal marriage or a presidential funeral is one of the major disappointments of the age.

Tax Regulations

Some criticism is leveled not so much against the regulation itself, but against the method of certificates, multiples, and price functions. It is argued that tax regulations might accomplish the same result. Since there is already a tax bureaucracy it is un-warranted to superimpose yet another Federal agency.

There are clear advantages to the use of taxes to regulate births. As a child is born, the taxrate of the family would be in-creased (rather than decreased, as at present) to compensate for externalities. One need not speculate on future earnings or in-heritances. The rich would pay more than the poor "automatically" in view of the progressive tax structure. The multitude of loopholes may make this thought somewhat fanciful, but loopholes can be plugged and anyway the tax can be organized more or less as a "head tax" and it can be related to the value of the house the family lives in rather than income. Head taxes have economic merit in that they do not affect the marginality conditions and thus are economically efficient, in particular when the tax is the same for all heads.

There are also clear disadvantages. For one thing, with taxes it will prove difficult if not impossible to regulate precisely. They are very difficult to "play" with for constitutional reasons, and reaction to them is hard to assess.

The main disadvantage is that once the child is there (or here) many parents need the money for proper rearing. This is indeed the sound reason why at present tax regulations favor the large families. Another disadvantage is the loss of psychological impact provided by the necessity to pay a lump sum for a certificate. Installment payments in the form of yearly taxes are much less effective on this score. Not for nothing does installment paying spur sales. Not for nothing does everyone know the price of a new car and no one the price of running a car for a year. The hospital bill for the maternity ward is precisely known, the cost of rearing a child is very vaguely perceived as positive.

Finally, taxes have two main uses—to get funds for the cost of government, and to regulate and mitigate economic cycles. To use the taxes also for the somewhat ulterior motive of regulating offspring would prove too hard a task. The success achieved in regulating economic activity, while certainly good enough to prevent another depression *à la* 1930, is not so stunning and secure as to warrant imposing yet another objective. The tightrope act of balancing acceptable rates of inflation with acceptable rates of unemployment is proving too much for economic acrobats and financial jugglers. It is unfair to ask them to perform their tricks while keeping their eyes on the birthrates.

Arbitrariness

The elements of arbitrariness in the plan are pointed out and challenged. For example, what if a family buys a certificate for a high price in view of high anticipated future earnings and then finds these anticipations wholly illusory? Many an expected inheritance proved a desert mirage. Do such families have recourse in the form of a refund?

The answer is that such regulations can rather easily be incorporated, although not without some rather substantial red tape and blossoming bureaucracy. The question then is whether they should be incorporated. This is doubtful. Life is very, very arbitrary to begin with. Not only is it wholly arbitrary where, to whom, and with what natural assets one is born, but it is also arbitrary in the monetary sense. Given ten accounts worth $10,000 on January 1, 1960, the value of these accounts will on January 1, 1975 range all the way from nothing to $100,000. These fluctuations completely swamp all conceivable arbitrariness in the administration of the birth regulation proposal. The arbitrariness is, of course, not quite fair, but fairness is not what life is all about. It is petulant to challenge this minor element of arbitrariness while living contentedly with all we already have.

It is, of course, possible to determine the multiple only as a function of current variables (current income and current net worth), but in a real sense that would create more arbitrariness, or at least unfairness, than addition of future related variables which are uncertain, as the future intrinsically is, but predictable within wide margins with high probability.

The Most Forceful Objection

In every crowd there are realists to point to the realities of the world we live in. They object, quite reasonably, that the world is not a rational world. They leave it at that, content to have scored a kill. Have they?

Jonah of whale-fame ("It is not that I cannot stand fish, fish cannot stand me") reluctantly went to Nineveh to preach impending doom. His admonitions were taken to heart, the city did penance for forty days and was saved from the ire of Gods. Jonah was sorely tested and bitterly disappointed in God's nonperformance, and indeed, it must be admitted, such a clear example of a self-non-fulfilling prophecy is relatively rare.

However, history teaches us what the Bible omits—that Jonah was only a little impatient. Not much more than a century later Nineveh was leveled in war, never to rise in glory again. Forty days of good behavior bought a century and some odd years. We are supposed to behave a lifetime for a payoff that may be less. Maybe, just maybe, we are quite realistic in not buying a proposal of this sort.

17

Global Population Control

Once Again, Three Criteria

The criteria of political acceptability, room for diversity, and organizational feasibility are equally as relevant for the global as for the national proposal.

The proposal must be politically acceptable by the majority of the global populace. It is to be understood, however, that the global majority will prevail even in those regions that handsomely defeat the proposal. Otherwise, those who refuse to comply reap the harvest without sharing in the cost of controlled behavior. To be politically acceptable, the proposal should leave some power to the national governments. It should also preclude the rich countries from buying out the birthrights of the poor countries.

Furthermore, the proposal should recognize diversity. It makes no sense to treat the poverty-stricken, drowning-prone inhabitants of the Ganges delta on the same basis as the energy-gobbling, pollution-spewing inhabitants of the Hudson shores.

Finally, the proposal should be organizationally feasible on a global basis, which is clearly a far more challenging problem than on a national basis.

Once Again, Certificates

Consider, then, the following proposal in the light of these criteria:

Certificates. Every woman, at age 15, is given two certificates in her name, each of which is good for the birth of one child. At age 30, she can sell the certificate to the global agency. This agency, in turn, will sell certificates in the name of those who want them.

Comment. There is nothing really new, apart from the fact that we now have a global agency. See, however, the next chapter for further elaboration.

Once Again, Multiples

Multiples. The following market structure is proposed. In a global bargaining session a multiple is established for each country. This multiple gives the ratio between buying price and selling price for inhabitants of that country. If a country has a multiple of 5, this would imply that the global agency would buy from its inhabitants at a certain price x, and sell to its inhabitants at 5 times that price, $5x$. The value x *should* rise if there is a net inflow of certificates to that country, and it *could* drop if there is a new outflow. The multiples are to be positively related to the prosperity of the nation concerned.

Comment. In this case the multiples pertain to countries, not to families. To fix ideas, the multiple for the United States could be 7, for Canada, Australia, New Zealand, Northern and Western Europe 5, for Russia, Japan, and Eastern Europe 4, for Middle and South America, Northern and Southern Africa, and East Asia 3, and so on—with appropriate exceptions for rich countries in poor regions and vice versa. The multiples are an extra levy on the rich. Their determination might be based on a formula, the GNP or some welfare index, and periodically updated using that formula. This would prevent continuous bargaining and bickering. Instead, one bargains just once to establish the formula.

Once Again, Prices

Prices. The multiple is established, by global agreement, but the prevailing price should be determined by the national countries themselves, within certain limits. No interference is called for when, at established prices, there is an equilibrium between demand and supply, or a net outflow of certificates. A net inflow of certificates, however, should only be permitted up to levels globally agreed upon as permissible for certain countries (Australia, for example), and then only if there is sufficient net outflow elsewhere.

Comment. As an example, let the multiple for the United States be 7, for the Netherlands 5, and for India 1½. The actual prices for buying and selling by inhabitants could be $3,500 and $500 (a ratio of 7) in the United States, the guilder equivalent of $2,000 and $400 (a ratio of 5) in the Netherlands, and the rupee equivalent of $60 and $40 (a ratio of 1½) in India. If, at these prices, the United States buys more certificates than it sells, prices should be raised to, perhaps, $4,900 and $700. This keeps the multiple at 7, as required. It would make buying less and selling certificates more attractive for Americans.

If Indian prices at $60 and $40 would roughly equal supply and demand, the Indian government could, nevertheless, raise prices to $90 and $60, which would result in a net outflow of certificates and a long-run population decline. Prices could not be lowered below the basic ratio, however, since that would result in a net inflow.

Once Again, Profits

Profits. The system is obviously exceedingly profitable. The profit should be used for free dispensing of pills and pro-phylactics to the poor, to help defray some medical costs, and, of course, for the administrative costs of running the agency.

Comment. If a country sets out on a course of deliberately diminishing its population, more certificates would be sold than bought, and this might lead to a net outflow of cash for the agency. If, at prices of $90 to buy and $60 to sell, 30 million Indians buy certificates and 50 million sell certificates, a quick calculation establishes a net monetary deficit of $300 million to the agency. This is not a trivial amount of "foreign aid."

Six Categories of Problems

Problems. The problems can be roughly grouped into six categories. In order of increasing importance those are problems of detail, problems of pricing, psychological problems, medical and ethical problems, organizational problems, and problems of acceptability.

Comment. The problems of detail are the same as before, although a greater variety of different customs, habits, beliefs, taboos, and superstitions will have to be allowed for, and some novel problems, such as adoption across the border and problems of migration in general must be tackled.

With respect to problems of *pricing*, it is basically the national government that will dictate the changes, although the government's hand will occasionally be forced, as when it is obliged to raise prices because of an influx of certificates. This poses the problem of definition or measurement of inflow and outflow. It is suggested that a price rise is called for if in any month the influx of certificates exceeds the outflow by more than 20 percent, or in any quarter by more than 10 percent, or in any year by more than 3 percent, or in any 3 years by more than 1 percent. Price decreases are allowed in reverse situations, but unlike increases they do not *have* to be implemented by the national governments, inasmuch as a deliberate decline in population may be desired by the country concerned. After some trial-and-error, prices would probably remain fairly stable. Current transactions should always be conducted at prevailing prices.

This is the place to repeat that if each woman were to receive not 2, but 2.3 certificates, the fraction could either be sold at the proportionate selling price (.3 certificates would sell for $150

if 1 sells for $500), or a fraction could be bought at the proportion-
ate buying price (.7 certificates would cost $2,450 if 1 certificate
cost $3,500). There is nothing holy about the number two.

The *psychological* problems are quite similar to those discussed above at the national level. For some societies the controls
hit harder than for others, as a function of national habits,
religions, and temperament. The Judaeo-Catholic philosophy will
not be helpful. Such asymmetry of pain is very regrettable, but
unavoidable.

Ethical and Organizational Problems

The *ethical* and *medical* problems for the uncertified birth of
a third child are as vexing as before. A penalty equal to the price
of a ticket will be hard to collect, and sterilization will, over and
above all moral objections, be hard to accomplish in a world where
50 percent of the population never sees a doctor. The best policing
here is peer and neighborhood pressure, since a child is hard to hide
and "If we cannot have three, why can they?" is the type of
question prone to set the juices of familial jealousy flowing at a
furious rate. Fear of social ostracism can be very effective.

There will remain villages high in the Andes, deep in
Australia's innards, or even perhaps settlements hidden in the
forests above a lazy loop of the Danube, where the procreation
proceeds apace with the past. So be it. Small slippage, provided it
goes largely unnoticed, will not defeat the system any more than
an occasional cadet cheating at exams defeats the honor code
system.

Organizational problems are, of course, vast, both within and
between countries. In the affluent West the system is eminently

feasible. In the poor nations, it will require immense effort even to explain the rules of the game, and it will be a herculean task to provide the necessary bureaucracy and doctors. On the other hand, there would be vast positive externalities for having such a system in operation, benefits far beyond the narrow scope of population control. Between nations the problem of mistrust, fear of cheating, and opposition to outside control are hurdles that must be overcome. Quite apart from all that, the system if implemented would do little to change the prevailing inequalities of population distribution. This is a very long-haul problem, to be solved peacefully only when the densely populated countries deliberately opt for fewer inhabitants.

In the computer age, the specific form of regulation proposed here appears feasible, not instantaneously everywhere, but on short notice in the high-multiple countries, which would create large sums of money that can be used to expand the program at a fast rate to gradually cover the whole globe within a decade. The bureaucracy and doctors or midwives would be paid for by the global community, and especially by the rich countries with high multiples. The rich countries would have no great edge if any over the poor countries. They could not help but export vast sums of money, not as a loan, or a gift, or a device to buy popularity, or an instrument in cold war policy, but as payment and recompensation for their dangerous, mean externalities. The self-financing aspect of the proposal is the largest organizational plus.

Political Acceptability

Problems of *political acceptability* are severe. This plan, however, has a lot to offer every country. Increased welfare for the poor nations, as well as the assurance that the rich could not buy out all the goodies the earth has in store. For the rich, there is the knowledge that their grandchildren may live to enjoy life, and the reward of knowing that, though poverty is here to stay, in view of its relativistic nature, it would not get any worse or more widespread.

Here again, there are many positive spillover effects. The feeling of global cohesiveness generated by common effort of population control, the prospect of mastering our own fate again instead of blindly climbing the exponentially rising slope, and the consequences of a more equitable distribution of wealth—those are the sentiments that might carry sufficient momentum to begin talking collectively and sensibly about pollution and resource depletion, about standards of quality rather than quantity of life, about an even more equitable distribution of the global pie, about moving from situations of conflict and aggression, segregation and discrimination to situations of competition and rivalry, cooperation and association, and about long-range planning aimed toward achieving a fairly constant number of literate, healthy, well-fed, and sheltered people, able to live a full life in decency and die with dignity after they have had their fill of it. Is that too much to expect from those who refer to themselves rather arrogantly as *homines sapientes*?

Not the least of the positive externalities would be the vastly diminished chance of nuclear episodes, since the *Lebensraum* problem will no longer intensify.

None of the problems we face can truly be solved without controlling population. We cannot afford waiting for nonexistent perfect solutions when we have imperfect existing solutions. As for the merits of the specific solution proposed here, consider the alternatives.

18

Meshing Global and National Schemes

Structure of the Problem

It is not obvious how the national schemes can fit into the global scheme. A global agency, as we saw, will establish one multiple for each nation and different multiples for different nations, for example, 7 for the United States, 5 for the Netherlands, and 1½ for India. The prices, by contrast, are to be determined nationally, in the normal case so as to equate on a national basis the demand and supply of certificates. This might mean U.S. buy-in and sell-out prices of $500 and $3,500, respectively, Dutch prices of $400 and $2,000, and Indian prices of $40 and $60. These prices are determined in such a way as to equilibrate import and export of certificates. They are, and this is the part where the shoe pinches, *uniform* for all nationals of each country.

A significant problem now arises when the national agency, in the interest of fairness and equity to its own nationals, employs its own multiple and price function scheme, for example as displayed in a numerical example in Chapter 15. This scheme leads to *different* prices for rich and poor. In that case the inhabitants of the nation will *only* be interested in their *own* multiples and prices. As we illustrated in Chapter 15, these can be constructed to equate demand and supply. The national agency gets rich in the process, and spends part of this covering its costs and possibly engaging in population control activities.

There is, of course, no problem if the national agency does not differentiate prices for its poor and rich inhabitants. It would then be easy to compute that to equate demand and supply for the United States, with its multiple of 7, would mean prices of $500 and $3,500. But these values *cannot* be found when the nation has organized its own segmented market, as seems the reasonable and decent thing to do.

Either-or Choice

The conclusion is that, once a global agency is operational, each nation has a choice. *Either*, it can proceed with constructing its own national multiple and price function market, and then the national agency will have to contribute all its surplus to the global agency. In this version the global multiple becomes inoperative. *Or* the country can work with unit prices for its inhabitants, in which case the global multiple is of essence. In that case the global agency clears $3,000 for every American buyer-and-seller pair in our numerical example.

In either case, once a global agency exists, all monies generated should go to the global agency. They would pay for all the legitimate bureaucratic costs of the national agency, plus all other activities it deems useful all over the globe, including organizing the bureaucracy, training the medical corps, and paying the bills in many less developed nations.

Reason for Global Approach

For any rich country, there are no apparent advantages for joining a global operation and for handing all its not-so-petty cash to this global agency. Even if the national operation might be deemed useful for its income redistribution features and to prevent the births of too many rich who pollute and poor who cannot pay, it is hard to see the advantage in tacking onto the global system and handling over all the cash.

From a selfish and short-run point of view, there is no such advantage. From a wider perspective, however, the advantage is that the U.S. funds generated by the proposal might induce other, poorer countries to control their populations by helping to pay for these controls. The *justification* is that the United States, or any other developed nation with a high multiple, is a very, very expensive, demanding citizen of the earth, producing a host of unfavorable externalities and depleting a multitude of resources. It should not shrink from its moral obligation to pay at least part of that bill with cold cash. Not as a gift, but as a pure and simple duty.

Common Globe or Global Commons

On the one hand, as argued in Chapter 16, it is not likely that national agencies will grow and prosper in the absence of a global attack on the population problem. The rich do not really need it, or so they may feel. The poor cannot really afford it, or so they may think. Many advantages accrue to those who do not regulate if others do.

On the other hand, even if there is a global agency the rich nations must have a truly perceptive eye for long-run interests of the globe as a whole, and a well-developed sense of fair play, to join the global effort. Such vision is not manifest at present.

Only an all-or-nothing implementation appears at all feasible. A half-hearted, feel-the-water with-your-toes approach cannot take off. The minimum critical amount of cooperation needed to make the proposal viable is quite large. It is here that we meet the real bottleneck. The social organization of the globe is too brittle.

The global social structure is based on selfishness, maintained by power-play, marred by short-run vision, and managed by crisis-hopping. The rich, while luxuriating in wealth, pay lip-service to serious problems shared by all, but lack inclination to act decisively. In the back of their minds they surely believe in the survival of the fittest. They are the fittest. The poor, distrustful of the rich, are so burdened with short-run survival that the long-run problems seem insignificant. To distract minds from the miseries at home, governments foster enemies abroad. Nothing makes for better cohesion than a common enemy.

The real common enemy is population. The whole globe has the same and common interest here: to keep it within limits. This could be the rallying point of the rich who deplete and the poor who starve alike, helping each other and thereby themselves, and creating in the process one globe, common to all. Instead, we are creating a global commons. We are dirtying and exhausting the only nest we have. It is a sad state of affairs. It is prone to self-destruct. It is small solace that, as a statistical certainty, there are thousands of other globes wandering through the universe.

Index